JAMES K. LOUTZENHISER

1/15/96 from Jane

THE SENSE AND SENSIBILITY

Screenplay & Diaries

THE SENSE AND SENSIBILITY

Screenplay & Diaries

Bringing Jane Austen's
Novel to Film

Emma Thompson

Photographs by Clive Coote
Introduction by Lindsay Doran

Newmarket Press
New York

ACKNOWLEDGEMENTS

I should like to acknowledge the profoundest debt for
my having developed any sense of humour to Jane Austen,
Monty Python and The Magic Roundabout

Introduction copyright © 1995 by Lindsay Doran. All rights reserved.
Diaries copyright © 1995 by Emma Thompson. All rights reserved.
Screenplay and all other text copyright © 1995 by Columbia Pictures Industries, Inc. All rights reserved.
Photographs by Clive Coote copyright © 1995 by Columbia Pictures Industries, Inc. All rights reserved.

This book published simultaneously in the United States of America and in Canada.

96 97 98 99   10 9 8 7 6 5 4 3 2 1

Library of Congress Cataloging-in-Publication Data

Thompson, Emma.
The Sense and sensibility screenplay and diaries : the making of the film based on the Jane Austen novel
/ Emma Thompson.
p. cm.
ISBN 1-55704-260-8
1. Sense and sensibility (Motion picture) I. Austen, Jane, 1775-1817. Sense and sensibility. II. Title.
PN1997.S36183T56   1995
791.43' 72—dc20

95-38999
CIP

Quantity Purchases

Companies, professional groups, clubs, and other organizations may qualify for special terms
when ordering quantities of this title. For information, write Special Sales,
Newmarket Press, 18 East 48th Street, New York, New York 10017, or call (212) 832-3575.

Book design by Bloomsbury Publishing, London.

First Edition

CONTENTS

LIST OF COLOUR ILLUSTRATIONS

INTRODUCTION

I F THERE WAS ANYTHING I knew for certain, it was that *Pride and Prejudice* was a very stupid book and that Jane Austen was a very stupid writer, and that I would never, ever read one of her stupid books again. I was thirteen years old.

I knew that *Pride and Prejudice* was supposed to be this big deal classic and everything, but I couldn't see anything great about it at all. It was about these five sisters who seemed to live for only one thing: visiting. The most important thing that could happen in their lives would be that somebody would drop by, or that they would drop by the home of somebody else, or best of all, that somebody new would move into the neighbourhood so there could be a whole new round of dropping by. That was it. They talked to each other, they talked to some men they met, then they talked to each other some more. Then they all got married, resulting in every single character becoming related to every single other character, and the book was over. Really stupid.

Mrs Ritter, who taught eighth grade at my all-girls' school, certainly meant well by assigning the book for us to read, but I think what she liked best about it was that it was safe stuff for young female minds. She certainly never attempted to communicate to us that it was full of wisdom and humour, and we were too young and too unsophisticated to figure it out for ourselves. At least I was. So I did my paper on what women wore in 1800 (the clothes, I reported to my friends, were almost as stupid as the book) and that, I thought, was the end of me and Jane Austen.

I was wrong. Five years later, when I was a freshman at Barnard College (another all-girls' school), I signed up for a class taught by a professor named John Kowenhoeven in which each student chose an English-speaking author and tried to read every single work of prose or poetry the author had written, in chronological order, without referring to critical essays or biographies. The point was not to get through all the writings (as I recall, the girl who chose Herman Melville never even got to *Moby Dick*), but to try to make our own judgements about the work of these authors without being influenced by what critics thought of it or what biographers implied had influenced it.

At the first class, we each presented the name of the author we wanted to study. I chose James Joyce (probably because some boy I once had a crush on thought that James Joyce was the Living God) and, after a few questions from Kowenhoeven, the choice was accepted. This was how it went for most of the students until one of them said that she intended to study Jane Austen. Everything stopped. It became clear rather quickly that Jane Austen was the author whom Professor Kowenhoeven most loved and admired, and he didn't think any of us was worthy of studying her. He grilled the poor student for what seemed like half an hour – why did she want to study Jane Austen? What books had she already read? What would she call the author in her term papers? ('Jane Austen' was the reply; it was clear that if the student had intended to refer to the author, even once, as 'Jane' or 'Miss Austen' or 'Ms Austen' or 'The Bard of Bath', Kowenhoeven would make her study someone else.) When question after question had been answered to his satisfaction, Kowenhoeven finally sat back in his chair, looked directly at (and somewhat through) the poor girl and said, 'Do you have a sense of humour?' 'For Jane Austen I have,' she replied with an equally level look. That did it. Her choice was accepted, and Kowenhoeven moved on to the girls who'd chosen to study Hardy, Woolf, Yeats, etc.

But I sat there stunned. I adored this professor (in spite of – or perhaps because of – being terrified of him), and I couldn't believe that he held Jane Austen in such high esteem. And the girl who had chosen to study Jane Austen (I don't remember her name, only her aura) struck me as being the coolest girl in the class – she had short dark curly hair when the rest of us were trying to look like Mary Travers from Peter, Paul and Mary, and she always brought a cello case to class. I couldn't figure it out – what did these people see in Jane Austen? And what did a sense of humour have to do with it? The only jokes I associated with Jane Austen were the childish ones I had made at her expense.

Once a week during the term, each student had to deliver an oral report on her chosen author to the rest of the class. Kowenhoeven was terribly hard on us after these reports ('I counted thirty-seven "y'know"s before I stopped counting,' he said to one girl; 'When you say "Joyce gives a good description" of something, what do you mean by "good"?' he said to me), yet he was surprisingly easy on the reports presented by the girl who had chosen to study Jane Austen. But it would have been impossible to be hard on them. They were brilliant. They were also thrilling, and above everything, they were hilarious.

The first pieces of writing by James Joyce that I'd come across were some school essays he'd written when he was about fifteen years old. They were rather dull, and didn't at all hint at the magic to come. The first pieces of Jane Austen we were treated to were some stories and plays she had written when she was a little younger than fifteen. We were all entranced by them, mostly because they were so wickedly funny. (Later Emma Thompson would comment to me that she thought Jane Austen's early works were more like Monty Python skits than anything else.)

As an illustration, here are some lines from the short tale 'Frederick and Elfrida', written when the author was much younger than any of us in that class (the spelling, grammar and punctuation are the author's own):

But e'er [Frederic, Elfrida and Charlotte] had been many minutes seated, the Wit and Charms which shone resplendent in the conversation of the amiable Rebecca, enchanted them so much that they all with one accord jumped up and exclaimed.

'Lovely and too charming Fair one, notwithstanding your forbidding Squint, your greazy tresses and your swelling Back, which are more frightfull than imagination can paint or pen describe, I cannot refrain from expressing my raptures, at the engaging Qualities of your Mind, which so amply atone for the Horror, with which your first appearance must ever inspire the unwary visitor.

'Your sentiments so nobly expressed on the different excel-

lencies of Indian and English Muslins, and the judicious preference you give the former, have excited in me an admiration of which I can alone give an adequate idea, by assuring you it is nearly equal to what I feel for myself.'

Over the course of the class, as we listened to Jane Austen's short works evolve into full-length novels, we not only laughed but marvelled at the careful crafting of her sentences, the intricacy of her story-telling, and the accuracy of her observations on human nature. Everyone looked forward to the days when the cellist gave her reports, while I don't remember anyone (including myself) looking forward to my attempts to explain Joyce's 'ineluctable modality of the visible'.

When the end of the school year came and the class was over, I was resolved that as soon as I could find enough free time, I would try to duplicate the steps of the cello player and read Jane Austen's works, every single one of them, in chronological order. But other interests and responsibilities intervened, and I wasn't able to fulfil my promise to myself until I was twenty-two and living for a year in England. Soon after I arrived there, when I was crossing the street near my flat in Earl's Court, I was hit by a very small car (probably because I was looking the wrong way). I was hurt just badly enough that I couldn't work, but not so badly that I couldn't limp to the neighbourhood library every morning and limp home every night. It was freezing cold in my flat so the library happily provided a warm alternative, and as I sat among the stacks trying to figure out what I wanted to read for the next few weeks, I suddenly remembered my resolution concerning the works of Jane Austen.

I went to the 'A' shelves and while they didn't contain everything Jane Austen had ever written, they did hold all the major novels. So, since my reading was to be chronological, I started with *Sense and Sensibility*. (I remembered from class that, although *Sense and Sensibility* had been published in 1811, it had been written in 1795 and was therefore the first of her novels.) Over the coming months I read the books in order all the way through to *Persuasion,* loving every one of them and cursing the dim-wittedness of my eighth-grade self, but as soon as I was finished I went back and re-read *Sense and Sensibility* which had emerged as my clear favourite, not only of Jane Austen's novels, but of all the novels I had ever read (fortunately, following Kowenhoeven's instructions, I hadn't read any criticism or biographies so I didn't find out till years later that I wasn't supposed to like *Sense and Sensibility* as much as I did).

Perhaps one of the reasons I loved that particular book so much was that it felt to me like a terrific movie. My father, D. A. Doran, had been a Hollywood studio executive for forty years and had passed on a lot of his ideas at the dinner table about what makes a satisfying film. Some of that information came in the form of simple rules such as 'Never advance the story by having a character say, "Why are you looking at me like that?" or "Why are you telling me all this?" ' But he also taught my brother Dan and me how to recognise the qualities in a book (or play or script) that would translate into a good film. And *Sense and Sensibility* seemed to have them all: wonderful characters, a strong love story (actually, *three* strong love stories), surprising plot twists, good jokes, relevant themes, and a heart-stopping ending. I decided right there, in the reading room of the Brompton Road Library, that if I ever went into the movie business (only a vague desire when I was twenty-two), I would try to make *Sense and Sensibility* into a film.

Eight years later that vague desire became a reality. I found myself working as an executive at a Hollywood studio and my first priority was still to make a movie out of my favourite book. That meant finding a screenwriter, and I felt I knew exactly what I was looking for: a writer who was equally strong in the areas of satire and romance (not an easy combination, I admit, since satirists are often too bitter to be romantic, and romantics are often too sentimental to be satiric); and a writer who was not only familiar with Jane Austen's language but who could *think* in that language almost as naturally as he or she could think in the language of the twentieth century. I knew that in order to translate Jane Austen's somewhat sprawling book into a riveting, cinematic tale, some scenes and dialogue would have to be altered or invented, and the tone and language of the new material would have to match the tone and language of the original. So I set to work, reading screenplays by writers who were both male and female, old and young, English and American.

Ten years later, I was still reading. Everything I'd looked at seemed so dry and polite – the romantic scripts weren't funny enough, the funny scripts weren't romantic enough, the attempts to write in the voice of the eighteenth century felt stilted and dull. I was beginning to think that what I was looking for didn't exist. But around that time, I took a new job running Sydney Pollack's production company Mirage. Sydney wanted Mirage to be a company that made movies based on our hearts' desires, not on whatever material happened to be submitted from the agencies. He and Mirage colleague Bill Horberg urged me not to give up, so once again I began to look.

The first movie I produced for Mirage was *Dead Again* starring Kenneth Branagh and Emma Thompson. I got to know Emma very well over the course of the twelve-week shoot, and it wasn't long before we discovered our mutual passion for Jane Austen. It was clear that she knew the books by heart, and that her appreciation of them was not of the dry, academic sort – she *enjoyed* them, and she loved their wit as much as she admired their intelligence. Also, she had had the good sense (and the satiric sensibility) to start loving Jane Austen's books when she was nine years old, long before she studied them in secondary school and at Cambridge University. (Once again, I thought back disdainfully to my thirteen-year-old self, but eventually I came to realise that Emma is so smart and talented in so many areas that she makes *everyone* feel inadequate. Have you ever seen her dance? Have you heard her speak French?)

As fate would have it, about two weeks into the *Dead Again* shooting schedule, the local PBS station KCET began airing the British television series that Emma had written called *Thompson*. The six half-hours consisted of a series of comic skits starring Emma, Ken, and a number of Emma's family and friends. My husband Rodney Kemerer and I found ourselves glued to it every week. Emma had told us that the British press, in their infinite wisdom, had dismissed the entire series, but we found it hilarious. In the first episode were two skits set in the past – in one of them Ken and Emma play Robin Hood and Maid Marian who are shown at a point in their relationship when the joys of living in the woods are wearing a bit thin. The second skit showed a Victorian mother's attempts to explain to her newly married daughter what the mouse-like creature was that had crawled out of her husband's trousers on their wedding night. The Victorian mouse skit was funny in exactly the ways that Jane Austen was funny, even though the subject matter was far more bawdy than what Jane Austen chose (or dared) to write about. And the Robin Hood skit was both funny and real, with a surprisingly romantic ending. Emma's ability to write in period language seemed effortless. In short, it was exactly the kind of writing I'd been searching for. I knew that Emma had never written a screenplay before, but there was enough sense of story-telling even in those two- and three-minute sketches to indicate that writing a full-length script wouldn't be too difficult a leap.

So when *Dead Again* was finished, Bill and I asked Emma if she would be interested in adapting *Sense and Sensibility* into a feature film. She seemed surprised by the choice of that book over certain other novels such as *Persuasion* or *Emma*, but eventually she came to share my feeling that *Sense and Sensibility* had more sheer entertainment value than the other books, and that it had the advantage of having two central female characters instead of the usual one. She agreed to try her hand at writing the script, but cautioned that she had 'one little movie' to act in first before she could begin. The little movie was *Howards End*.

In the next few months, while Emma was in England giving the performance that would win her an Oscar the following year, Sydney and I went around Hollywood trying to find a studio that would put up the money for a 200-year-old English novel to be adapted by an untried screenwriter who was also, at that time and place, a little-known actress ('Does she have to be *in* it?' lamented one studio executive who eventually turned the project down.) But

13

Amy Pascal and Gareth Wigan at Columbia Pictures saw the light. We showed them the first episode of *Thompson* which they adored, and we convinced them that *Sense and Sensibility*, while considered one of Jane Austen's 'lesser novels' (to this day, I don't understand that), would make a rich and entertaining film.

Emma took the role of screenwriter seriously from the beginning. She not only knew how to think in Jane Austen's language, but she understood the rhythms of good scene writing and how to convey a sense of setting. Like all good screenwriters ('What do you mean by "good"?' asks Professor Kowenhoeven in my head), she didn't object to rewriting a scene again and again when it was required, and she wasn't afraid to cut a line or a scene or a series of scenes when she saw that they weren't working. Her experience as an actress served her well when it came to writing clever and efficient dialogue (you'll notice that no character says 'Why are you looking at me like that?' or 'Why are you telling me all this?' even though there are ample opportunities for them to do so), but it also helped her to understand when silence could say more than any spoken word.

In the years that followed, Emma would make a film and write a draft, make a film and write a draft, over and over again. Sometimes she'd make a film and write three drafts. Through it all, there were notes from Columbia and notes from Mirage. The Columbia executives were particularly (and rightly) concerned that we keep the story focused on the relationship between the two sisters so that it wouldn't seem like a movie about a couple of women waiting around for men. And Sydney was ever vigilant about making the language and values of the late eighteenth century accessible to the average twentieth-century movie-goer. At one point he said to me, 'You're too close to all this, Lindsay. You know the book too well. Most people won't even know that Norland Park and Barton Park are houses – they'll think they're brothers.'

But eventually, after Emma had appeared in seven films and had written probably twice that many drafts, we had a script we were ready to show to directors. And now a new search began – where would we find a director who displayed that same mixture of satire and romance that had been so hard to find in a writer? How long would we have to look this time? While Sydney, Bill and I were trying to figure out who could direct Emma's script (most people assumed we would confine our search to English directors, women directors, or English women directors), our newest Mirage colleague, Geoff Stier, was becoming a devotee of a Taiwanese director named Ang Lee. Geoff was the first of us at Mirage to see Ang's film *The Wedding Banquet*, and he told the rest of us that we should take a look at it right away and consider Ang for some of the projects we had in development at Mirage. Sydney was the next one to see it, and as he and Geoff talked enthusiastically about Ang's work, there were two words which kept coming up – 'funny' and 'romantic'. It was a familiar combination.

Bill and I saw *The Wedding Banquet* soon afterwards, and then it became a matter of which of us had the nerve to suggest the idea first: a Taiwanese director for *Sense and Sensibility*? Were we crazy? (Later Ang said, 'When I opened the script and saw Jane Austen's name on the title page, I thought you guys were crazy.') But when we saw Ang's next film, *Eat Drink Man Woman*, the idea of combining Ang Lee and Jane Austen became even more appealing. After all, *Eat Drink Man Woman* was a story of sisters, and it contained elements of both satire and romance. It even contained some of the same dialogue, word for word, as *Sense and Sensibility* (in both films, one sister says to another in an uncharacteristic moment of anger, 'What do you know of my heart?')

So we submitted the script to Ang's agent. And then we held our breath.

Two weeks later we received a call saying that Ang wanted to meet with us about the script, and it turned out to be the meeting we'd been dreaming of. Not only did he appreciate the script's humour, but he said, 'I want this film to break people's hearts so badly they'll still be recovering from it two months later.' And he spoke of the deep meaning that the title held for him – Sense and Sensibility, two elements that represent the core of life itself, like Yin and Yang, or Eat, Drink, Man, Woman. Ang was not a student of Jane Austen (although James Schamus, his co-producer and frequent co-writer,

---

15

knows her work intimately), but he immediately recognised the universality of this story and of these characters.

So Ang signed on to be the director of *Sense and Sensibility*, and his first act as director was to ask Emma if she would play the part of Elinor Dashwood. This was an idea that Mirage and Columbia had been encouraging for some time, and Emma graciously agreed to accept the role.

So now we had our script, we had our director, and we had our star – it was time to make a movie. The first part of the *Sense and Sensibility* journey – the process of finding a writer, developing a screenplay, and then finding a director – took fifteen years. The rest of the journey – the actual making of the film – is recorded in Emma's diaries which are presented here along with the shooting draft of her screenplay.

Our fondest hope is that people who love Jane Austen will find the film to be faithful to the humour and wisdom of the original novel, but we also hope that the film will be a satisfying and entertaining experience for people who have never read any Jane Austen novels at all, or who *have* read the novels, but thought they were stupid. If there's just one thirteen-year-old girl who sees the film and afterwards decides to revise her opinion of Jane Austen, that's good enough for me.

Lindsay Doran, *Producer*

The CAST

ELINOR DASHWOOD
Emma Thompson

EDWARD FERRARS
Hugh Grant

COLONEL BRANDON
Alan Rickman

MARIANNE DASHWOOD
Kate Winslet

MRS DASHWOOD
Gemma Jones

MARGARET DASHWOOD
Emilie François

LUCY STEELE
Imogen Stubbs

MR PALMER
Hugh Laurie
CHARLOTTE PALMER
Imelda Staunton

FANNY DASHWOOD *Harriet Walter*
JOHN DASHWOOD *James Fleet*

JOHN WILLOUGHBY
Greg Wise

SIR JOHN MIDDLETON *Robert Hardy*
MRS JENNINGS *Elizabeth Spriggs*

ROBERT FERRARS
Richard Lumsden

The SCREENPLAY

ABBREVIATIONS

CAM	camera
cont.	continued
CU	close-up
ECU	extreme close-up
EVE	evening
EXT	exterior
INT	interior
POV	point of view
V/O	voice-over

Note: Gaps in the numbering of scenes are due to the omission of some scenes during filming.

0 EXT. OPEN ROADS. NIGHT. TITLE SEQUENCE.
A series of travelling shots. A well-dressed, pompous-looking individual (JOHN DASHWOOD, 35) is making an urgent journey on horseback. He looks anxious.

1 EXT. NORLAND PARK. ENGLAND. MARCH 1800. NIGHT.
Silence. Norland Park, a large country house built in the early part of the eighteenth century, lies in the moonlit parkland.

2 INT. NORLAND PARK. MR DASHWOOD'S BEDROOM. NIGHT.
In the dim light shed by candles we see a bed in which a MAN (MR DASHWOOD, 52) lies – his skin waxy, his breathing laboured. Around him two silhouettes move and murmur, their clothing susurrating in the deathly hush. DOCTORS. A WOMAN (MRS DASHWOOD, 50) sits by his side, holding his hand, her eyes never leaving his face.

> MR DASHWOOD (*urgent*)
> Is John not yet arrived?

> MRS DASHWOOD
> We expect him at any moment, dearest.

MR DASHWOOD *looks anguished.*

> MR DASHWOOD
> The girls – I have left so little.

> MRS DASHWOOD
> Shh, hush, Henry.

> MR DASHWOOD
> Elinor will try to look after you all, but make sure she finds a good husband. The men are such noodles hereabouts, little wonder none has pleased her.

They smile at each other. MRS DASHWOOD is just managing to conceal her fear and grief.

> MRS DASHWOOD
> But Marianne is sure to find her storybook hero.

> MR DASHWOOD
> A romantic poet with flashing eyes and empty pockets?

> MRS DASHWOOD
> As long as she loves him, who*ever* he is.

> MR DASHWOOD
> Margaret will go to sea and become a pirate so we need not concern ourselves with her.

MRS DASHWOOD *tries to laugh but it emerges as a sob. An older* MANSERVANT (THOMAS) *now enters, anxiety written on every feature.*

> THOMAS
> Your son is arrived from London, sir.

MR DASHWOOD *squeezes his wife's hand.*

> MR DASHWOOD
> Let me speak to John alone.

She nods quickly and he smiles at her with infinite tenderness.

> MR DASHWOOD
> Ah, my dear. How happy you have made me.

MRS DASHWOOD *makes a superhuman effort and smiles back. She allows* THOMAS *to help her out. She passes* JOHN DASHWOOD *as he enters, presses his hand, but cannot speak.* JOHN *takes her place by the bed.*

> JOHN
> Father . . .

MR DASHWOOD *summons his last ounces of energy and starts to whisper with desperate intensity.*

MR DASHWOOD

John – you will find out soon enough from my will that the estate of Norland was left to me in such a way as prevents me from dividing it between my families.

JOHN *blinks. He cannot quite take it in.*

JOHN

Calm yourself, Father. This is not good for you –

But MR DASHWOOD *continues with even greater determination.*

MR DASHWOOD

Norland in its entirety is therefore yours by law and I am happy for you and Fanny.

JOHN *looks torn between genuine distress and unexpected delight.*

MR DASHWOOD

But your stepmother – my wife – and daughters are left with only five hundred pounds a year, barely enough to live on and nothing for the girls' dowries. You must help them.

JOHN*'s face is a picture of conflicting emotions. Behind them is the ominous rustling of parchments.*

JOHN

Of course –

MR DASHWOOD

You must promise to do this.

A brief moment of sincerity overcomes JOHN*'s natural hypocrisy.*

JOHN

I promise, Father, I promise.

MR DASHWOOD *seems relieved. Suddenly his breathing changes.* JOHN *looks alarmed. He rises and we hear him going to find the* DOCTOR.

––––––––

                    JOHN
        Come! Come quickly!

But it is we who share the dying man's last words.

                 MR DASHWOOD
        Help them . . .

3 EXT. JOHN AND FANNY'S TOWN HOUSE. LONDON. DAY.
*Outside the house sits a very well-to-do carriage. Behind it waits another
open carriage upon which servants are laying trunks and boxes.*

                  FANNY (V/O)
        'Help them?'

4 INT. JOHN AND FANNY'S TOWN HOUSE. DRESSING ROOM. DAY.
JOHN *is standing in mourning clothes and a travelling cape. He is watching,
and obviously waiting for, a pert* WOMAN (FANNY DASHWOOD) *who is
standing by a mirror looking at him keenly.*

                    FANNY
        What do you mean, 'help them'?

                    JOHN
        Dearest, I mean to give them three thousand pounds.

FANNY *goes very still.* JOHN *gets nervous.*

                    JOHN
        The interest will provide them with a little extra income. Such a
        gift will certainly discharge my promise to my father.

FANNY *slowly turns back to the mirror.*

                    FANNY
        Oh, without question! More than amply . . .

                    JOHN
        One had rather, on such occasions, do too much than too little.

                    ————

A pause as FANNY *turns and looks at him again.*

JOHN

Of course, he did not stipulate a particular sum . . .

5 INT. LAUNDRY. NORLAND PARK. DAY.
A red-eyed MAID (BETSY) *plunges a beautiful muslin frock into a vat of black dye.*

6 INT. NORLAND PARK. MRS DASHWOOD'S BEDROOM. DAY.
MRS DASHWOOD *is rushing about, mourning ribbons flapping, putting her knick-knacks into a small valise. The room is in chaos. A young* WOMAN (ELINOR DASHWOOD) *looks on helplessly.*

MRS DASHWOOD

To be reduced to the condition of visitor in my own home! It is not to be borne, Elinor!

ELINOR

Consider, Mamma! We have nowhere to go.

MRS DASHWOOD

John and Fanny will descend from London at any moment, followed no doubt by cartloads of relatives ready to turn us out of our rooms one by one – do you expect me to be here to welcome them? Vultures!

She suddenly collapses into a chair and bursts into tears.

ELINOR

I shall start making enquiries for a new house at once. Until then we must try to bear their coming.

7 INT. JOHN AND FANNY'S CARRIAGE. DAY.
JOHN *and* FANNY *are on their way out of London.*

JOHN

Fifteen hundred then. What say you to fifteen hundred?

_____

FANNY

What brother on earth would do half so much for his real sisters
– let alone half-blood?

JOHN

They can hardly expect more.

FANNY

There is no knowing what they expect. The question is, what
can you afford?

8 INT. NORLAND PARK. DRAWING ROOM. DAY.
A beautiful young WOMAN (MARIANNE DASHWOOD) *is sitting at the
piano playing a particularly sad piece.* ELINOR *enters.*

ELINOR

Marianne, cannot you play something else? Mamma has been
weeping since breakfast.

MARIANNE *stops, turns the pages of her music book and starts playing
something equally lugubrious.*

ELINOR

I meant something less mournful, dearest.

9 EXT. ROADSIDE INN. DAY.
JOHN *and* FANNY *are waiting as the* OSTLERS *make the final adjustments
to their carriage. The* LANDLORD *hovers, waiting for a tip.*

JOHN

A hundred pounds a year to their mother while she lives. Would
that be more advisable? It is better than parting with the fifteen
hundred all at once.

He displays some coins in his hand. FANNY *removes one and nods.*

FANNY

But if she should live longer than fifteen years we would be

———

33

completely taken in. People always live forever when there is an annuity to be paid them.

JOHN *gives the coins to the* LANDLORD.

10 EXT. NORLAND PARK. MARGARET'S TREE-HOUSE. DAY.
ELINOR *comes to the foot of a large tree from which a small staircase issues.*

> ELINOR
> Margaret, are you there? Please come down. John and Fanny will be here soon.

A pause. ELINOR *is about to leave when a disembodied and truculent young voice stops her.*

> MARGARET (V/O)
> Why are they coming to live at Norland? They already have a house in London.

> ELINOR
> Because houses go from father to son, dearest – not from father to daughter. It is the law.

Silence. ELINOR *tries another tack.*

> ELINOR
> If you come inside, we could play with your atlas.

> MARGARET (V/O)
> It's not my atlas any more. It's their atlas.

CLOSE *on* ELINOR *as she ponders the truth of this statement.*

11 INT. JOHN AND FANNY'S CARRIAGE. DAY.
JOHN *and* FANNY *joggle on.*

> JOHN
> Twenty pounds now and then will amply discharge my promise, you are quite right.

FANNY

Indeed. Although to say the truth, I am convinced within myself that your father had no idea of your giving them money.

JOHN

They will have five hundred a year amongst them as it is –

FANNY

– and what on earth can four women want for more than that? Their housekeeping will be nothing at all – they will have no carriage, no horses, hardly any servants and will keep no company. Only conceive how comfortable they will be!

12 INT. NORLAND PARK. SERVANTS' HALL. DAY.
The large contingent of SERVANTS *who staff Norland Park are gathered in gloomy silence as* ELINOR *addresses them.*

ELINOR

As you know, we are looking for a new home. When we leave we shall be able to retain only Thomas and Betsy.

CAM *holds on* THOMAS *and* BETSY, *a capable woman.*

ELINOR (*cont.*)

We are very sorry to have to leave you all. But we are certain you will find the new Mrs Dashwood a fair and generous mistress.

13 EXT. NORLAND PARK. DRIVE. DAY.
JOHN *and* FANNY's *carriage approaches Norland.*

FANNY (V/O)

They will be much more able to give *you* something.

14 INT. JOHN AND FANNY'S CARRIAGE. DAY.
JOHN *and* FANNY *are about to get out.*

———

JOHN

So – we are agreed. No money – but the occasional gift of game and fish in season will be very welcome.

FANNY

Your father would be proud of you.

15 INT. NORLAND PARK. DINING ROOM. EARLY EVE.
The entire family, with the exception of MARGARET, is present. BETSY is serving food in an atmosphere of stiff silence. Cutlery clinks. JOHN chews loudly. MARIANNE is rigid with resentment. MRS DASHWOOD maintains a cool, removed dignity. ELINOR tries to play hostess.

ELINOR

How is Mrs Ferrars?

FANNY

My mother is always in excellent health, thank you. My brother Robert is in town with her this season and quite the most popular bachelor in London! He has his own barouche.

In the brief silence which follows this, FANNY surreptitiously checks the hallmark on her butterknife.

ELINOR

You have two brothers, have you not?

FANNY

Indeed, yes. Edward is the eldest – Mamma quite depends upon him. He is travelling up from Plymouth shortly and will break his journey here.

MRS DASHWOOD *looks at* ELINOR *pointedly.* JOHN *notices.*

JOHN (*to* MRS DASHWOOD)

If that is agreeable to you, of course.

———

36

MRS DASHWOOD

My dear John – this is *your* home now.

FANNY *looks about, barely able to conceal her satisfaction.*

16 INT. NORLAND PARK. ELINOR'S BEDROOM. DAY.
ELINOR *is sitting with a little pile of parcels. She puts a shawl into some paper and ties it with ribbon as* MARIANNE *thunders in, looking mutinous.*

MARIANNE

Fanny wishes to know where the key for the silver cabinet is kept.

ELINOR

Betsy has it, I think. What does Fanny want with the silver?

MARIANNE

I can only presume she wants to count it. What are you doing?

ELINOR

Presents for the servants. Have you seen Margaret? I am worried about her. She has taken to hiding in the oddest places.

MARIANNE

Fortunate girl. At least she can escape Fanny, which is more than any of us is able.

ELINOR

You do your best. You have not said a word to her for a week.

MARIANNE (*truculently*)

I have! I have said 'yes' and 'no'.

17 INT. NORLAND PARK. BREAKFAST ROOM. DAY.
FANNY, MRS DASHWOOD, ELINOR *and* JOHN *are at breakfast.* MARIANNE *enters.* ELINOR *catches her eye and indicates* FANNY *with a slight motion of her head.* MARIANNE *makes a face.*

MARIANNE (*very polite*)

Good morning, Fanny.

———

FANNY *is rather startled.*

> FANNY
> Good morning, Marianne.

ELINOR *is relieved.*

> MARIANNE (*to Fanny*)
> How did you find the silver? Is it all genuine?

ELINOR *rushes in before* MARIANNE *gets any further.*

> ELINOR
> Pray, when may we expect the pleasure of your brother's company?

> FANNY
> Edward is due tomorrow. And my dear Mrs Dashwood, in view of the fact that he will not be with us for long, I wondered if Miss Margaret would mind giving up her room to him – the view is quite incomparable from her windows and I should so much like Edward to see Norland at its best.

MARIANNE *slams her cup down and throws a furious look at* ELINOR.

18 INT. NORLAND PARK. MARGARET'S BEDROOM. DAY.
ELINOR *and* MARIANNE *are removing* MARGARET'*s toys.*

> MARIANNE
> Intolerable woman!

> ELINOR
> There is but one consolation – if Edward is anything like Fanny, we shall be only too happy to leave.

19 EXT. NORLAND PARK. DRIVE. DAY.
A very capable HORSEMAN (EDWARD FERRARS) *canters up the gravel drive. CLOSE on his face as he gazes up at the elegant façade.*

20 INT. NORLAND PARK. DRAWING ROOM. DAY.

Everyone except MARGARET is present. EDWARD has just shaken hands with ELINOR. He behaves with great respect to the DASHWOODS and seems embarrassed by FANNY's proprietorial air.

FANNY

But where is Miss Margaret? I declare, Mrs Dashwood, I am beginning to doubt of her existence! She must run positively wild!

MRS DASHWOOD

Forgive us, Mr Ferrars. My youngest is not to be found this morning. She is a little shy of strangers at present.

EDWARD

Naturally. I am also shy of strangers and I have nothing like her excuse.

MARIANNE (*dangerous*)

How do you like your view, Mr Ferrars?

ELINOR glances at her warningly but EDWARD replies with careful consideration.

EDWARD

Very much. Your stables are very handsome and beautifully kept, Mrs Dashwood.

FANNY

Stables! Edward – your windows overlook the lake.

EDWARD

An – oversight, Fanny, led me to the wrong room. I have rectified the situation and am happily settled in the guest quarters.

MARIANNE and ELINOR look at each other in surprise. FANNY looks furious. MRS DASHWOOD *smiles warmly at* EDWARD. CLOSE *on* ELINOR. *She is impressed.*

21 INT. NORLAND PARK. STAIRCASE. DAY.
FANNY *is walking with* EDWARD, *who looks at the pictures with interest.*

> FANNY
> They are all exceedingly spoilt, I find. Miss Margaret spends all her time up trees and under furniture and I have barely had a civil word from Marianne.

> EDWARD
> My dear Fanny, they have just lost their father – their lives will never be the same again.

> FANNY
> That is no excuse.

22 INT. NORLAND PARK. LIBRARY. DAY.
FANNY *leads* EDWARD *in. She sniffs with distaste.*

> FANNY
> I have never liked the smell of books.

> EDWARD
> Oh? No. The dust, perhaps.

As they speak, EDWARD *notices a large atlas retreating apparently all by itself across the floor. Someone is obviously under the table, pulling it out of sight. He registers it and immediately moves in such a way as to shield it from* FANNY. *He turns back, searching for something to divert her.*

> EDWARD
> I hear you have great plans for the walnut grove.

> FANNY
> Oh yes! I shall have it pulled down to make room for a Grecian temple.

There is a stifled wail from under the table, which EDWARD covers with a cough.

> EDWARD
>
> How picturesque. Will you show me the site?

And he ushers FANNY out, flicking a quick glance over his shoulder at the fugitive's foot.

23 INT. NORLAND PARK. VELVET ROOM. DAY.
ELINOR, MRS DASHWOOD *and* MARIANNE *are sitting round a table with a pile of letters.* ELINOR *is handing one back to her mother.*

> ELINOR
>
> Too expensive. We do not need four bedrooms, we can share.

> MARIANNE
>
> This one, then?

ELINOR *reads the letter quickly.*

> ELINOR
>
> Marianne, we have only five hundred pounds a year. I will send out more enquiries today.

There is a knock on the door. Hesitantly, EDWARD *appears.*

> EDWARD
>
> Pardon my intrusion, but I believe I have found what you are looking for . . .

MARIANNE *and* MRS DASHWOOD *are puzzled by his elliptical manner but* ELINOR *immediately understands and rises, in smiling relief.*

24 INT. NORLAND PARK. ENTRANCE HALL OUTSIDE LIBRARY.
DAY.
EDWARD *is standing outside keeping a discreet lookout. The door is half open and he can hear* ELINOR *trying to coax* MARGARET *out.* FANNY *walks by with a* BUTLER *to whom she is giving instructions.* EDWARD

pretends to examine the mouldings and she passes on unsuspecting.

ELINOR (V/O)
Won't you come out, dearest? We haven't seen you all day.
Mamma is very concerned.

More silence. EDWARD *thinks hard. He makes a decision.*

25 INT. NORLAND PARK. LIBRARY. DAY.
EDWARD *walks in loudly.*

EDWARD
Oh, Miss Dashwood! Excuse me – I was wondering – do you by
any chance have such a thing as a reliable atlas?

ELINOR *looks up at him in astonishment.*

ELINOR
I believe so.

EDWARD
Excellent. I wish to check the position of the Nile.

EDWARD *appears to be utterly sincere.*

EDWARD
My sister says it is in South America.

From under the table we hear a snort. ELINOR *looks at him in realisation.*

ELINOR
Oh! No, no indeed. She is quite wrong. For I believe it is in – in –
Belgium.

EDWARD
Belgium? Surely not. You must be thinking of the Volga.

MARGARET (*from under the table*)
The Volga?

———

43

ELINOR

Of course. The Volga, which, as you know, starts in –

EDWARD

Vladivostok, and ends in –

ELINOR

St Albans.

EDWARD

Indeed. Where the coffee beans come from . . .

They are having such a good time that it is rather a pity the game is stopped by the appearance from under the table of MARGARET who reveals herself to be a dishevelled girl of eleven. She hauls the atlas up and plonks it in front of EDWARD.

MARGARET

The source of the Nile is in Abyssinia.

EDWARD

Is it? Good heavens. How do you do. Edward Ferrars.

MARGARET

Margaret Dashwood.

EDWARD *shakes* MARGARET's *hand solemnly and looks over her head at* ELINOR. *They smile at each other, a connection made.*

26 INT. NORLAND PARK. DRAWING ROOM. ANOTHER DAY.
JOHN *is reading a newspaper.* MRS DASHWOOD *sits across from* FANNY, *who thumbs through a fashion-plate magazine.* ELINOR *is at a desk by the window writing a letter – we see the words 'of course we should like to leave as soon as possible'. Suddenly she hears a commotion outside.* MARGARET *runs past the window brandishing a stick.* EDWARD *follows, and proceeds to teach her the first principles of sword-fighting. They feint and parry,* EDWARD *serious and without a hint of condescension,* MAR-

GARET *concentrating furiously.* EDWARD *suddenly turns, as though feeling* ELINOR's *gaze. She smiles but looks away quickly.*

27 INT. NORLAND PARK. VELVET ROOM. ANOTHER DAY.

EDWARD *comes into the doorway and sees* ELINOR *who is listening to* MARIANNE *playing a concerto.* ELINOR *stands in a graceful, rather sad attitude, her back to us. Suddenly she senses* EDWARD *behind her and turns. He is about to turn away, embarrassed to have been caught admiring her, when he sees she has been weeping. Hastily she tries to dry her eyes. He comes forward and offers her a handkerchief, which she takes with a grateful smile. We notice his monogram in the corner: ECF.*

> ELINOR (*apologetic*)
> That was my father's favourite.

EDWARD *nods kindly.*

> ELINOR
> Thank you so much for your help with Margaret, Mr Ferrars. She is a changed girl since your arrival.

> EDWARD
> Not at all. I enjoy her company.

> ELINOR
> Has she shown you her tree-house?

> EDWARD
> Not yet. Would you do me the honour, Miss Dashwood? It is very fine out.

> ELINOR
> With pleasure.

They start to walk out of shot, still talking.

> ELINOR
> Margaret has always wanted to travel.

––––––

EDWARD

I know. She is heading an expedition to China shortly. I am to go as her servant but only on the understanding that I will be very badly treated.

ELINOR

What will your duties be?

EDWARD

Sword-fighting, administering rum and swabbing.

ELINOR

Ah.

CAM *tilts up to find* MRS DASHWOOD *on the middle landing of the staircase, smiling down at them.* CAM *tilts up yet further to find* FANNY *on the landing above, watching* EDWARD *and* ELINOR *with a face like a prune.*

28 EXT. NORLAND PARK. GARDENS. DAY.
EDWARD *and* ELINOR *are still talking as they walk arm in arm in the late-afternoon sun.*

EDWARD

All I want – all I have ever wanted – is the quiet of a private life but my mother is determined to see me distinguished.

ELINOR

As?

EDWARD

She hardly knows. Any fine figure will suit – a great orator, a leading politician, even a barrister would serve, but only on the condition that I drive my own barouche and dine in the first circles.

His tone is light but there is an underlying bitterness to it.

———

ELINOR

And what do you wish for?

EDWARD

I always preferred the church, but that is not smart enough for
my mother – she prefers the army, but that is a great deal too
smart for me.

ELINOR

Would you stay in London?

EDWARD

I hate London. No peace. A country living is my ideal – a small
parish where I might do some good, keep chickens and give very
short sermons.

30 EXT. FIELDS NEAR NORLAND. DAY.
EDWARD *and* ELINOR *are on horseback. The atmosphere is intimate, the
quality of the conversation rooted now in their affections.*

ELINOR

You talk of feeling idle and useless – imagine how that is
compounded when one has no choice and no hope whatsoever
of any occupation.

EDWARD *nods and smiles at the irony of it.*

EDWARD

Our circumstances are therefore precisely the same.

ELINOR

Except that you will inherit your fortune.

He looks at her slightly shocked but enjoying her boldness.

ELINOR (*cont.*)

We cannot even earn ours.

                              EDWARD
Perhaps Margaret is right.

                              ELINOR
Right?

                              EDWARD
Piracy is our only option.

They ride on in silence for a moment.

                         EDWARD (*cont.*)
What *is* swabbing exactly?

31 INT. NORLAND PARK. DRAWING ROOM. EVE.
Dinner is over. JOHN *and* FANNY *are examining plans of the Norland estate, looking for somewhere to build a hermitage.* EDWARD *is reading out loud.* ELINOR *embroiders and listens.* MRS DASHWOOD *and* MAR-IANNE *make up the rest of the audience, the latter in a state of high impatience.*

                              EDWARD
No voice divine the storm allayed
No light propitious shone,
When snatched from all effectual aid,
We perished each alone:
But I beneath a rougher sea,
And whelmed in deeper gulfs than he.

MARIANNE *jumps up and goes to him.*

                             MARIANNE
No, Edward! Listen –

She takes the book from him and reads the stanza with passionate brio.

                             MARIANNE
Can you not feel his despair? Try again.

Rather mortified, EDWARD *starts again, but not before receiving a sympathetic look from* ELINOR *which seems to comfort him a little.*

32 INT. NORLAND PARK. MORNING ROOM. DAY
MRS DASHWOOD *is ruminating sadly.* MARIANNE *rushes in holding a letter.*

> MARIANNE
> Mamma, look. This has just arrived.

> MRS DASHWOOD (*reading from the letter*)
> 'I should be pleased to offer you a home at Barton Cottage as soon as ever you have need of it' – why, it is from my cousin, Sir John Middleton!

> MARIANNE
> Even Elinor must approve the rent.

MRS DASHWOOD *looks at the letter again and thinks.*

> MRS DASHWOOD
> Has Elinor not yet seen this?

> MARIANNE
> No – I will fetch her.

> MRS DASHWOOD
> Wait. No. Let us delay.

> MARIANNE
> Why?

> MRS DASHWOOD
> I think – I believe – that Edward and Elinor have formed an attachment.

Marianne nods, a little reluctantly.

51

MRS DASHWOOD
It would be cruel to take her away so soon – and Devonshire is so far.

MRS DASHWOOD *makes her decision. She takes the letter and hides it in the pocket of her gown.* MARIANNE *looks on frowningly.*

MRS DASHWOOD
Why so grave? Do you disapprove her choice?

MARIANNE
By no means. Edward is very amiable.

MRS DASHWOOD
Amiable – but?

MARIANNE
But there is something wanting. He is too sedate – his reading last night . . .

MRS DASHWOOD
Elinor has not your feelings, his reserve suits her.

MARIANNE *thinks for a little.*

MARIANNE
Can he love her? Can the ardour of the soul really be satisfied with such polite, concealed affections? To love is to burn – to be on fire, all made of passion, of adoration, of sacrifice! Like Juliet, or Guinevere or Heloïse –

MRS DASHWOOD
They made rather pathetic ends, dear.

MARIANNE
Pathetic! To die for love? How can you say so? What could be more glorious?

52

MRS DASHWOOD

I think that may be taking your romantic sensibilities a little far . . .

MARIANNE

The more I know of the world, the more I am convinced that I shall never see a man whom I can truly love.

MRS DASHWOOD

You require so much!

MARIANNE

I do not! I require only what any young woman of taste should – a man who sings well, dances admirably, rides bravely, reads with passion and whose tastes agree in every point with my own.

33 INT. NORLAND PARK. ELINOR'S BEDROOM. NIGHT.

ELINOR *is in bed, deep in thought.* MARIANNE *enters in her nightclothes, carrying a book of poetry. She reads, teasingly.*

MARIANNE

Is love a fancy, or a feeling? No
It is immortal as immaculate truth
'Tis not a blossom shed as soon as Youth
Drops from the stem of life – for it will grow
In barren regions, where no waters flow
Nor ray of promise cheats the pensive gloom –

She jumps onto the bed. ELINOR *smiles – somewhat suspiciously.*

MARIANNE

What a pity it is that Edward has no passion for reading.

ELINOR

It was you who asked him to read – and then you made him nervous.

———

                    MARIANNE
Me?

                    ELINOR
But your behaviour to him in all other respects is perfectly cordial
so I must assume that you like him in spite of his deficiencies.

              MARIANNE (*trying hard*)
I think him everything that is amiable and worthy.

                    ELINOR
Praise indeed!

                    MARIANNE
But he shall have my unanswering devotion when you tell me he
is to be my brother . . .

ELINOR *is greatly taken aback and does not know how to reply. Suddenly*
MARIANNE *hugs her passionately.*

                    MARIANNE
How shall I do without you?

                    ELINOR
Do without me?

MARIANNE *pulls away, her eyes full of tears.*

                    MARIANNE
I am sure you will be very happy. But you must promise not to
live *too* far away.

                    ELINOR
Marianne, there is no question of – that is, there is no understanding between . . .

ELINOR *trails off.* MARIANNE *looks at her keenly.*

                    MARIANNE
Do you love him?

———

The bold clarity of this question discomforts ELINOR.

> ELINOR
> I do not attempt to deny that I think very highly of him – that I greatly esteem – that I *like* him.

> MARIANNE
> Esteem him! Like him! Use those insipid words again and I shall leave the room this instant!

This makes ELINOR *laugh in spite of her discomfort.*

> ELINOR
> Very well. Forgive me. Believe my feelings to be stronger than I have declared – but further than that you must not believe.

MARIANNE *is flummoxed but she rallies swiftly and picks up her book again.*

> MARIANNE
> 'Is love a fancy or a feeling?' Or a Ferrars?

> ELINOR
> Go to bed!

ELINOR *blushes in good earnest.* MARIANNE *goes to the door.*

> MARIANNE (*imitating Elinor*)
> 'I do not attempt to deny that I think highly of him – greatly esteem him! Like him!'

And she is gone, leaving ELINOR *both agitated and amused.*

34 INT. NORLAND PARK. BREAKFAST ROOM. DAY.
FANNY *is standing by the window looking out. We see her POV of* ELINOR *and* EDWARD *walking in the garden.* MRS DASHWOOD *enters, pauses for a moment and then joins* FANNY *at the window.* FANNY *pretends not to have been watching but* MRS DASHWOOD *looks down at the lovers and then smiles sweetly at her.*

––––––

MRS DASHWOOD

We are all so happy that you chose to invite Edward to Norland. He is a dear boy and we are all very fond of him.

FANNY *does a bit of quick thinking.*

FANNY

We have great hopes for him. Much is expected of him by our mother with regard to his profession –

MRS DASHWOOD

Naturally.

FANNY

And in marriage. She is determined that both he and Robert will marry well.

MRS DASHWOOD

Of course. But I hope she desires them to marry for love, first and foremost? I have always felt that, contrary to common wisdom, true affection is by far the most valuable dowry.

FANNY

Love is all very well, but unfortunately we cannot always rely on the heart to lead us in the most suitable directions.

FANNY *lowers her voice confidingly.*

FANNY

You see, my dear Mrs Dashwood, Edward is entirely the kind of compassionate person upon whom penniless women can prey – and having entered into any kind of understanding, he would never go back on his word. He is quite simply incapable of doing so. But it would lead to his ruin. I worry for him so, Mrs Dashwood. My mother has always made it perfectly plain that she will withdraw all financial support from Edward, should he choose to plant his affections in less . . . exalted ground than he deserves.

It is impossible for MRS DASHWOOD *not to get the point. She is appalled and furious.*

MRS DASHWOOD

I understand you perfectly.

She sweeps off.

35 INT. NORLAND PARK. MRS DASHWOOD'S DRESSING ROOM. DAY.

MRS DASHWOOD, *breathless with rage, is searching through her wardrobe for the gown which contains* SIR JOHN's *letter. Frocks fly hither and thither. Finally* MRS DASHWOOD *plunges her hand into the right pocket and withdraws the letter. She looks at it, suddenly concerned and anxious.*

---

36 INT. NORLAND PARK. DINING ROOM. EVE.
The entire family is present. Everyone is watching MRS DASHWOOD, *who has just made her announcement.*

                    EDWARD
Devonshire!

He is devastated. FANNY *is thrilled.* MRS DASHWOOD *looks at him with compassion and then at* ELINOR, *who is trying to keep calm.*

                    MRS DASHWOOD
My cousin Sir John Middleton has offered us a small house on his estate.

                    JOHN
Sir John Middleton? What is his situation? He must be a man of property.

                    MRS DASHWOOD
He is a widower. He lives with his mother-in-law at Barton Park and it is Barton Cottage that he offers us.

                    FANNY
Oh, a cottage! How charming. A little cottage is always very snug.

                    EDWARD
But you will not leave before the summer?

                    MRS DASHWOOD
Oh, my dear Edward, we can no longer trespass upon your sister's good will. We must leave as soon as possible.

                    MARGARET
You will come and stay with us, Edward!

                    EDWARD
I should like that very much.

FANNY

Edward has long been expected in town by our mother.

MRS DASHWOOD *ignores* FANNY.

MRS DASHWOOD

Come as soon as you can, Edward. Remember that you are always welcome.

37 INT/EXT. NORLAND PARK. STABLES. DAY.

ELINOR *has come to say goodbye to her* HORSE. *She strokes the soft face sadly. Then she senses someone and turns to find* EDWARD *standing nearby.*

EDWARD

Cannot you take him with you?

————

ELINOR

We cannot possibly afford him.

EDWARD

Perhaps he could make himself useful in the kitchen?

ELINOR *tries to smile.* EDWARD *looks at her for a long moment and then comes closer.*

EDWARD

Miss Dashwood – Elinor. I must talk to you.

The use of her Christian name – and in such a loving tone – stops ELINOR's *breath altogether.*

EDWARD

There is something of great importance I need . . . to tell you –

He comes closer still. The HORSE *breathes between them.* ELINOR *is on fire with anticipation but* EDWARD *looks troubled and has less the air of a suitor than he might.*

EDWARD

– about – about my education.

ELINOR (*after a beat*)

Your education?

EDWARD

Yes. It was less . . . successful than it might have been.

EDWARD *laughs nervously.* ELINOR *is completely bewildered.*

EDWARD

It was conducted in Plymouth – oddly enough.

ELINOR

Indeed?

                    EDWARD
Yes. Do you know it?

                    ELINOR
Plymouth?

                    EDWARD
Yes.

                    ELINOR
No.

                    EDWARD
Oh – well – I spent four years there – at a school run by a – a Mr
Pratt –

                    ELINOR
Pratt?

ELINOR *is beginning to feel like a parrot.*

                    EDWARD
Precisely – Mr Pratt – and there, I – that is to say, he has a –

As EDWARD *flounders, a familiar voice cuts through this unexpected foray
into his academic past.*

                    FANNY
Edward! Edward!

They turn to find FANNY *powering down upon them, waving a letter.*
EDWARD *steps back, glancing almost guiltily at* ELINOR, *who is as
confused as we are.*

                    FANNY
I have been all over for you! You are needed in London this instant!

                    EDWARD
Fanny, I am leaving this afternoon as it is –

———

FANNY

No, no, that will not do. Family affairs are in chaos owing to your absence. Mother is quite adamant that you should leave at once.

FANNY *is determined. She obviously has no intention of leaving him alone with* ELINOR. EDWARD *turns to* ELINOR, *frustration in every muscle, his jaw set tight.*

EDWARD

Excuse me, Miss Dashwood.

FANNY *drags* EDWARD *off, leaving* ELINOR *to gaze sadly after them.*

39 INT. THE LADIES' CARRIAGE. OPEN ROAD. RAIN. EVE.
The DASHWOODS *are on their way. The mood is very sombre.*

MARGARET

Edward promised he would bring the atlas to Barton for me.

MARIANNE *looks at* ELINOR, *pleased.*

MARIANNE

Did he? Well, I will wager he will do so in less than a fortnight!

MRS DASHWOOD *looks at* ELINOR *with satisfaction.*

40 EXT. THE LADIES' CARRIAGE. OPEN ROAD. EVE.
The carriage rolls on.

MARGARET (V/O)

Are we there yet?

41 EXT. ROAD TO AND FROM BARTON COTTAGE. DAY.
In comparison to Norland, Barton Cottage has the air of a damp shoebox. It sits low and bleak in the grey lonely countryside.

From one side we can see the DASHWOODS' *carriage drawing up at the gate. From the other, a much grander vehicle, from which loud whooping can be heard, is approaching.*

42 EXT. BARTON COTTAGE. GARDEN PATH. DAY.

As the exhausted DASHWOODS *alight, they converge with a ruddy-complexioned* MAN *in a redingote* (SIR JOHN MIDDLETON) *and a rotund, equally roseate* LADY (MRS JENNINGS) *who have fallen over each other in their haste to get out of their carriage.*

> MRS DASHWOOD
> Sir John!

SIR JOHN *clasps her hands and starts to help her up the path, followed by* ELINOR, MARIANNE *and* MARGARET, *who is clearly fascinated by his bouncy companion.*

> SIR JOHN
> Dear ladies, dear ladies, upon my word, here you are, here you are, here you are!

MRS DASHWOOD

Sir John, your extraordinary kindness –

SIR JOHN

Oh, none of that, hush, please, none of that, but here is my dear mamma-in-law Mrs Jennings.

MRS JENNINGS

Was the journey tolerable, you poor souls?

SIR JOHN

Why did you not come up to the Park first and take your ease? We saw you pass –

Like many people who live rather lonely lives together, SIR JOHN and MRS JENNINGS talk incessantly, interrupt each other all the time and never listen.

MRS JENNINGS

– but I would not wait for you to come to us, I made John call for the carriage –

SIR JOHN

She would not wait, you know.

MRS JENNINGS

– as we get so little company.

They reach the front door and BETSY's smiling welcome. In the confusion of milling people and THOMAS carrying the lighter luggage, MARIANNE contrives to slip into the house alone. We follow her but hear the conversation continuing in V/O. MARIANNE looks about the parlour, where a dismal fire is smoking. She starts up the stairs, expressionless.

MRS JENNINGS (V/O)

But I feel as if I know you already – delightful creatures!

3

4

5

6

9

10

14

16

SIR JOHN (V/O)

Delightful! And you know you are to dine at Barton Park every day.

MRS DASHWOOD (V/O)

Oh, but dear Sir John, we cannot –

SIR JOHN (V/O)

Oh, no no no no no no no, I shall not brook refusals. I am quite deaf to 'em, you know –

MRS JENNINGS (V/O)

– deaf –

MARIANNE *enters a small bedroom. She sits on the bed. Then she goes to the window and opens it. Voices float up.*

SIR JOHN (V/O)

But I insist!

ELINOR (V/O)

Let us only settle in for a few days, Sir John, and thank you –

SIR JOHN (V/O)

Oh, no thankings, no, please, can't bear 'em, embarrassing, you know –

MARIANNE *closes the window and crosses the corridor to another bedroom – similarly stark. She sighs and turns back down the stairs.*

SIR JOHN (V/O)

We will send game and fruit as a matter of course –

MRS JENNINGS (V/O)

– fruit and game –

SIR JOHN (V/O)

– and the carriage is at your beck and call –

MARIANNE *joins the group, who are now in the parlour.*

MRS JENNINGS

– call – and here is Miss Marianne!

SIR JOHN

Where did you disappear to?

MRS JENNINGS

I declare you are the loveliest girl I ever set eyes on! Cannot you get them married, Mrs Dashwood? You must not leave it too long!

SIR JOHN

But, alas, there are no smart young men hereabouts to woo them –

MRS JENNINGS

– not a beau for miles!

The strain of exhibiting joy and gratitude is beginning to tell on MRS DASHWOOD *who is sagging visibly.*

SIR JOHN

Come, Mother, let us leave them in peace.

MRS JENNINGS

But there is Colonel Brandon!

SIR JOHN *is dragging her down the path.*

SIR JOHN

Excellent fellow! We served in the East India Regiment together.

MRS JENNINGS

Just wait till he sees you! If we can persuade him out to meet you!

———

SIR JOHN

Reclusive individual. But you are fatigued. I can see that you are
fatigued.

Now he is pushing her into the carriage.

MRS JENNINGS

Of course she is fatigued!

SIR JOHN

Come along, Mother, we really must leave them to themselves.

MRS JENNINGS

You must get your maidservant to make you up some camphor
– it is the best tonic for the staggers!

SIR JOHN

Send Thomas to us for the carriage when you are ready!

*They take off, waving wildly. MARGARET goes down the path to watch
them and turns back to her slightly stunned family.*

MARGARET

I like *them.*

MRS DASHWOOD (*weakly*)

What generosity.

ELINOR

Indeed. I am surprised they did not offer us their clothing.

43 INT. BARTON COTTAGE. ELINOR AND MARIANNE'S
BEDROOM. NIGHT.
MARIANNE *and* ELINOR *are getting undressed for bed. It's very cold.
They keep their underclothing on and get in, shivering at the bony chill of the
linen.*

44 EXT. BARTON COTTAGE. KITCHEN GARDEN. DAY.
BETSY *is pinning out laundry.*

---

45 EXT. BARTON COTTAGE. GARDEN. DAY.
MARGARET *tries to climb an impossible tree. Her petticoats snag and tear.*

46 INT. BARTON COTTAGE. ELINOR AND MARIANNE'S
BEDROOM. DAY.
MARIANNE *looks out of the window at the wild countryside. Unconsciously, one hand plays up and down on the sill as though it were a keyboard.*

47 INT. BARTON COTTAGE. PARLOUR. DAY.
ELINOR *sits at a little desk counting money and making notes.* BETSY *enters to clean out the fire. She notices the money.*

                    BETSY
        Sugar is five shilling a pound these parts, Miss Dashwood.

                ELINOR (*lightly*)
            No more sugar then.

48 INT. BARTON COTTAGE. PARLOUR. EVE.
CLOSE *on* MRS DASHWOOD *looking out of the window, thinking. She remembers* MRS JENNINGS's *words:*

                MRS JENNINGS (V/O)
            Not a beau for miles . . .

MRS DASHWOOD *turns into the room to look at her brood.* ELINOR *and* MARIANNE *are mending* MARGARET's *petticoats.* CLOSE *on the mother's anxious expression – what is to become of them?*

49 EXT. BARTON PARK. EVE.
Establishing shot of SIR JOHN's *house – a very comfortable-looking country seat with fine grounds.*

                SIR JOHN (V/O)
        Where can Brandon be, poor fellow? I hope he has not lamed his
        horse.

---

50 INT. BARTON PARK. DINING ROOM. EVE.

CLOSE *on an empty chair and place setting. Pull out to reveal the* DASH-
WOODS *at their first dinner with* SIR JOHN *and* MRS JENNINGS.

> MRS JENNINGS
>
> Colonel Brandon is the most eligible bachelor in the county – he
> is bound to do for one of you. Mind, he is a better age for Miss
> Dashwood – but I dare say she left her heart behind in Sussex,
> eh?

MARIANNE *flashes an unmistakable glance of alarmed concern at her
sister, which* MRS JENNINGS *notices.*

> MRS JENNINGS
>
> Aha! I see you, Miss Marianne! I think I have unearthed a
> secret!

> SIR JOHN
>
> Oho! Have you sniffed one out already, Mother? You are worse
> than my best pointer, Flossie!

They both laugh immoderately. ELINOR *tries to stay calm.*

> MRS JENNINGS
>
> What sort of man is he, Miss Dashwood? Is he butcher, baker,
> candlestick-maker? I shall winkle it out of you somehow, you
> know!

> SIR JOHN
>
> She's horribly good at winkling.

> MRS JENNINGS
>
> You are in lonely country now, Miss Dashwood, none of us has
> any secrets here –

> SIR JOHN
>
> – or if we do, we do not keep them for long!

———

ELINOR *tries to smile.* MARIANNE *looks furious.* MARGARET *is staring at* MRS JENNINGS *as if she were some particularly thrilling form of wildlife.*

MRS JENNINGS
He is curate of the parish, I dare say!

SIR JOHN
Or a handsome lieutenant!

MRS JENNINGS
Give us a clue, Miss Dashwood – is he in uniform?

ELINOR *starts to change the subject, but* MARGARET *interrupts her.*

MARGARET
He has no profession!

SIR JOHN *and* MRS JENNINGS *turn on her with screams of delight.* ELINOR, MARIANNE *and* MRS DASHWOOD *look at each other helplessly.*

SIR JOHN
No profession! A gentleman, then!

MARIANNE (*with daggers*)
Margaret, you know perfectly well there is no such person.

MARGARET
There is! There is! And his name begins with an F!

ELINOR *looks hard at her plate.*

MRS DASHWOOD
Margaret!

MRS DASHWOOD *is appalled at her youngest's relish for such a vulgar game.* SIR JOHN *and* MRS JENNINGS *are cock-a-hoop.*

SIR JOHN
F indeed! A very promising letter. Let me – F, F, Fo, Fa . . . Upon my word, but I cannot think of a single name beginning with F –

MRS JENNINGS
Forrest? Foster? Frost? Foggarty?

MARIANNE *suddenly stands up.* SIR JOHN *and* MRS JENNINGS *are so surprised they stop talking. Everyone stares at* MARIANNE.

MARIANNE (*controlled fury*)
Sir John, might I play your pianoforte?

SIR JOHN
Of course, yes – my goodness. We do not stand on ceremony here, my dear.

For once, ELINOR *is grateful for her sister's rudeness as everyone rises and follows* MARIANNE *out.*

51 EXT. BARTON PARK. FRONT STEPS. EVE.
A soldierly MAN *of about forty* (COLONEL BRANDON) *is dismounting from his horse. From within we hear* MARIANNE's *song begin. His head snaps up to the windows. An expression of pained surprise comes into his melancholy, brooding eyes.*

52 INT. BARTON PARK. MUSIC ROOM. EVE.
Everyone watches MARIANNE *as she plays and sings. Behind them we see* BRANDON *entering. But he stays in the shadow of the door and no one notices him.* CLOSE *on his face. He gazes at* MARIANNE *with an unfathomable look of grief and longing. He breathes in deeply. Suddenly,* ELINOR *feels his presence and looks around at him. After a few moments, she turns back, slightly puzzled. The song finishes. Everyone claps. The* MAN *ventures out into the light and* SIR JOHN *springs from his seat.*

SIR JOHN
Brandon! Where have you been? Come, come and meet our beautiful new neighbours!

MRS JENNINGS
What a pity you are late, Colonel! You have missed the most delightful singing!

BRANDON *bows to the company and smiles slightly.*

>COLONEL BRANDON
>A great pity, indeed.

ELINOR *looks at him, even more puzzled.*

>SIR JOHN
>Mrs Dashwood, may I present my dear friend Colonel Brandon? We served together in the East Indies and I assure you there is no better fellow on earth –

>MARGARET
>Have you really been to the East Indies, Colonel?

>COLONEL BRANDON
>I have.

>MARGARET
>What is it like?

MARGARET *is quivering with fascination.*

>SIR JOHN
>Like? Hot.

But COLONEL BRANDON *knows what* MARGARET *wants to hear.*

>COLONEL BRANDON (*mysteriously*)
>The air is full of spices.

MARGARET *smiles with satisfaction.*

>SIR JOHN
>Come, Miss Dashwood – it is your turn to entertain us!

>ELINOR
>Oh no, Sir John, I do not –

SIR JOHN
– and I think we can all guess what key you will sing in!

SIR JOHN *and* MRS JENNINGS *are bursting with their new joke.*

SIR JOHN/MRS JENNINGS
F major!

They fall about.

53 INT. SIR JOHN'S CARRIAGE. NIGHT.
The DASHWOODS *are returning home. A row is in progress.*

MARIANNE (*to Margaret*)
As for you, you have no right, no right at all, to parade your
ignorant assumptions –

MARGARET
They are not assumptions. You *told* me.

ELINOR *stares at* MARIANNE. MARIANNE *colours and attacks* MAR-
GARET *again.*

MARIANNE
I told you nothing –

MARGARET
They'll *meet* him when he comes, anyway.

MARIANNE
That is not the point. You do not speak of such things before
strangers –

MARGARET
But everyone *else* was –

MARIANNE
Mrs Jennings is not everyone.

————

> MARGARET
>
> I like her! She talks about things. We never talk about things.

> MRS DASHWOOD
>
> Hush, please, now that is enough, Margaret. If you cannot think of anything appropriate to say, you will please restrict your remarks to the weather.

A *heated pause.*

> MARGARET
>
> I like Colonel Brandon too. He's been to places.

54 EXT. POND NEAR BARTON PARK. DAY.

In the background, SIR JOHN, ELINOR and MRS JENNINGS pack the remains of a picnic into a basket. MRS DASHWOOD and MARGARET examine a foxhole. In the foreground, MARIANNE is cutting bulrushes for

basketwork. Her knife is blunt and she saws impatiently. COLONEL BRANDON *materialises at her side and wordlessly offers her his hunting knife. Oddly nervous,* MARIANNE *takes it. She turns back to the rushes and cuts them with ease. The* COLONEL's *gaze follows her movements as if held by a magnet.*

54A INT. KEEPER'S LODGE. BARTON PARK. DAY.
SIR JOHN *and* BRANDON *are cleaning their guns in companionable silence – a habit left over from army days.* SIR JOHN *eyes* BRANDON *roguishly.*

> SIR JOHN
> You know what they're saying, of course . . .

No answer.

> SIR JOHN
> The word is that you have developed a taste for – certain company . . .

BRANDON *stays resolutely silent.* SIR JOHN *is emboldened.*

> SIR JOHN
> And why not, say I. A man like you – in his prime – she'd be a most fortunate young lady –

BRANDON *cuts across him.*

> COLONEL BRANDON
> Marianne Dashwood would no more think of me than she would of *you*, John.

> SIR JOHN
> Brandon, my boy, do not think of yourself so meanly –

> COLONEL BRANDON
> And all the better for her.

SIR JOHN *subsides.* BRANDON *is clearly as angry with himself as he is with* SIR JOHN.

54B EXT. POND NEAR BARTON PARK. ANOTHER DAY.
BRANDON *strides along in hunting gear, a gun slung under one arm, his dog trotting behind him with a duck clamped between its jaws. The bulrushes catch his eye and he slows, then stops. He stands for a moment deep in thought. Then he takes his hunting knife, cuts one and walks off contemplatively.*

57 EXT. BARTON PARK. GARDENS. DAY.
An outdoor luncheon is in progress. COLONEL BRANDON *is talking to* MRS DASHWOOD. *Occasionally he looks over towards* MARIANNE, *who is playing bilboquet with* SIR JOHN *and* MARGARET. MRS JENNINGS *nudges* ELINOR *hard and gestures to* BRANDON.

MRS JENNINGS (*stage whisper*)

Besotted! Excellent match, for *he* is rich and *she* is handsome.

ELINOR

How long have you known the Colonel?

MRS JENNINGS

Oh, Lord bless you, as long as ever I have been here, and I came fifteen years back. His estate at Delaford is but four miles hence and he and John are very thick. He has no wife or children of his own, for –

MRS JENNINGS *lowers her voice to a stentorian whisper.*

MRS JENNINGS

– he has a tragic history. He loved a girl once – twenty years ago now – a ward to his family, but they were not permitted to marry . . .

ELINOR *is intrigued.*

ELINOR

On what grounds?

MRS JENNINGS
Money. Eliza was poor. When the father discovered their amour, she was flung out of the house and he packed off into the army. I believe he would have done himself a harm if not for John . . .

ELINOR
What became of the lady?

MRS JENNINGS
Oh, she was passed from man to man – disappeared from all good society. When Brandon got back from India he searched for heaven knows how long, only to find her dying in a poorhouse. You have seen how it has affected him. Once I thought my daughter Charlotte might have cheered him up, but she is much better off where she is.

ELINOR *is silent with amazement at this unexpected history.*

MRS JENNINGS
Look at him *now*, though. So attentive. I shall try an experiment on him.

ELINOR
Oh no, please, dear Mrs Jennings, leave the poor Colonel alone.

MRS JENNINGS
No, no, it is just the thing – all suitors need a little help, my dear . . .

MRS JENNINGS *winks at* ELINOR *and rubs her hands as though about to perform a magic trick.*

MRS JENNINGS (*trillingly*)
Colonel Brandon!

BRANDON *looks up.*

MRS JENNINGS
We have not heard you play for us of late!

COLONEL BRANDON
For the simple reason that you have a far superior musician here.

He indicates MARIANNE, *who smiles absently.*

MRS JENNINGS
Perhaps you did not know, Miss Marianne, that our dear Brandon shares your passion for music and plays the piano-forte very well.

MARIANNE *looks at* BRANDON *in some surprise.*

MRS JENNINGS
Play us a duet!

BRANDON *looks at* MRS JENNINGS *warningly but she ignores him.*

MRS JENNINGS
I'll trow you know quite as many melancholy tunes as Miss Marianne!

Her tone is so knowing that MARIANNE *frowns uncomfortably.*

MRS JENNINGS
Come! Let us see you both side by side!

MARIANNE *rises impatiently.*

MARIANNE
I do not know any duets. Forgive me, Colonel.

She moves away. MRS JENNINGS *chuckles.*

58 INT. BARTON COTTAGE. PARLOUR. LATE AFTERNOON.
The DASHWOODS *returning.* MARIANNE *is taking her bonnet off so furiously that she simply gets the knot tighter and tighter. Despite themselves,* ELINOR *and* MRS DASHWOOD *are amused.*

MARIANNE

Oh! Are we never to have a moment's peace? The rent here may be low but I think we have it on very hard terms . . .

ELINOR

Mrs Jennings is a wealthy woman with a married daughter – she has nothing to do but marry off everyone else's.

BETSY *pokes her head out from the dining room.*

BETSY

There's a parcel arrived for you, Miss Dashwood!

MARGARET

A parcel!

They all crowd into the dining room to find a large package on the table, which MARGARET is permitted to open. In the meantime ELINOR comes to the rescue with the bonnet and MARIANNE stands shifting like a spirited mare as ELINOR patiently unravels the knot.

MARIANNE

It is too ridiculous! When is a man to be safe from such wit if age and infirmity do not protect him?

ELINOR

Infirmity!

MRS DASHWOOD

If Colonel Brandon is infirm, then I am at death's door.

ELINOR

It is a miracle your life has extended this far . . .

MARIANNE

Did you not hear him complain of a rheumatism in his shoulder?

ELINOR

'A slight ache' I believe was his phrase . . .

———

79

MARIANNE *smiles and* ELINOR *laughs at her. Then* MARGARET *opens the parcel to reveal – her atlas. The atmosphere alters immediately as* MRS DASHWOOD *and* MARIANNE *look at* ELINOR *in consternation.*

> MARGARET
> But Edward said he would bring it himself.

There is a letter on top of the atlas. CLOSE *on the address 'To the Dashwoods'.* MRS DASHWOOD *picks it up, looks at* ELINOR, *and opens it.*

> MRS DASHWOOD
> 'Dear Mrs Dashwood, Miss Dashwood, Miss Marianne and Captain Margaret – it gives me great pleasure to restore this atlas to its rightful owner. Alas, business in London does not permit me to accompany it, although this is likely to hurt me far more than it hurts you. For the present my memories of your kindness must be enough to sustain me, and I remain your devoted servant always. E. C. Ferrars.'

A silence greets this brief epistle. ELINOR *struggles to contain her bitter disappointment.*

> MARGARET
> But why hasn't he come?

> MRS DASHWOOD
> He says he is busy, dear.

> MARGARET
> He *said* he'd come.

MARGARET *is genuinely upset.* ELINOR *quietly hangs up* MARIANNE's *bonnet.*

> MARGARET
> Why hasn't he come?

MRS DASHWOOD *looks beseechingly at* MARIANNE, *who nods and grasps* MARGARET's *hand.*

MARIANNE

I am taking you for a walk.

MARGARET

No! I've been a walk.

MARIANNE

You need another.

MARGARET

It is going to rain.

MARIANNE *shoves her bonnet back on and drags* MARGARET *out.*

MARIANNE

It is not going to rain.

MARGARET

You always say that and then it always does.

We hear the front door slam behind them. There is a short silence.

MRS DASHWOOD

I fear Mrs Jennings is a bad influence.

She approaches ELINOR.

MRS DASHWOOD

You must miss him, Elinor.

ELINOR *looks very directly at her mother.*

ELINOR

We are not engaged, Mamma.

MRS DASHWOOD

But he loves you, dearest, of that I am certain.

———

ELINOR *looks down. She speaks slowly, choosing her words with care.*

ELINOR

I am by no means *assured* of his regard for me.

MRS DASHWOOD

Oh, Elinor!

ELINOR

But even were he to feel such a . . . preference, I think we should be foolish to assume that there would not be many obstacles to his choosing a woman of no rank who cannot afford to buy sugar . . .

MRS DASHWOOD

But Elinor – your heart must tell you –

ELINOR

In such a situation, Mamma, it is perhaps better to use one's head.

She clears her throat, rises determinedly, picks up the accounts book and opens it. MRS DASHWOOD *is silenced.*

58A EXT. FIELDS NEAR BARTON COTTAGE. DAY.
MARIANNE *walks very briskly, dragging an unwilling* MARGARET *behind her.*

59 EXT. DOWNS NEAR BARTON COTTAGE. DAY.
It has started to rain. Mists are gathering around the two figures walking against the wind.

MARIANNE

Is there any felicity in the world superior to this?

MARGARET

I told you it would rain.

MARIANNE

Look! There is some blue sky! Let us chase it!

———

MARGARET

I'm not supposed to run . . .

MARIANNE *runs off down the hill into the heart of the mist.* MARGARET *stumbles after her, grumbling. We follow* MARIANNE *in her headlong descent and suddenly, dramatically, she trips and sprawls to the ground, letting out a sharp cry of pain.*

MARGARET

Marianne!

MARIANNE

Help me!

She tries to get up, but the pain in her ankle is too great. She sinks back to the ground. MARGARET *is very alarmed.*

MARIANNE

Margaret, run home and fetch help.

The mists have thickened. They can no longer see where they are. Despite her rising fear, MARGARET *squares her shoulders bravely and tries to sense the direction.*

MARGARET

I think it is this way. I will run as fast as I can, Marianne.

She dashes off. As she goes into the mist we hear the thunder of hooves. CU Margaret's terrified expression. They seem to be coming from all around. She wheels and turns and then – Crash! Through the mist breaks a huge white horse. Astride sits an Adonis in hunting gear. MARGARET *squeals. The horse rears.* Its rider *controls it and slides off. He rushes to* MARIANNE's *side.*

THE STRANGER

Are you hurt?

MARIANNE (*transfixed*)

Only my ankle.

THE STRANGER
May I have your permission to –

He indicates her leg. Decorous, perhaps faintly impish.

THE STRANGER
– ascertain if there are any breaks?

MARIANNE *nods speechlessly. With great delicacy, he feels her ankle.*
MARGARET's *eyes are out on chapel-hooks.* MARIANNE *almost swoons
with embarrassment and excitement mixed.*

THE STRANGER
It is not broken. Now, can you put your arm about my neck?

MARIANNE *does not need any encouragement. He lifts her effortlessly and
calls to his horse: 'Bedivere!' It trots obediently forward. The* STRANGER
smiles down at MARIANNE.

THE STRANGER
Allow me to escort you home.

60 INT. BARTON COTTAGE. DINING ROOM. DAY.
Rain is thudding against the window from which MRS DASHWOOD *turns, looking very worried.*

MRS DASHWOOD
Marianne was sure it would not rain.

ELINOR
Which invariably means it *will*.

But we can see she is trying to conceal her anxiety from her mother. There are noises in the hall.

MRS DASHWOOD
At last!

MARGARET *runs into the room dripping wet.*

MARGARET
She fell over! She fell down – and he's carrying her!

61 INT. BARTON COTTAGE. FRONT DOOR. DAY.
MRS DASHWOOD *and* ELINOR *rush to the front door. They see the* STRANGER *carrying* MARIANNE *up the garden path, his scarlet coat staining the monochrome rain.*

MRS DASHWOOD
Marianne!

The STRANGER *reaches the door. This is no time for introductions.*

ELINOR
In here, sir – this way. Margaret, open the door wider. Please, sir, lay her here. Marianne, are you in pain?

They move into the parlour.

———

62 INT. BARTON COTTAGE. PARLOUR. DAY.
MARIANNE *is carried in, surrounded by* ELINOR, MRS DASHWOOD *and* MARGARET.

>   THE STRANGER
>   It is a twisted ankle.

>   MARIANNE
>   Do not be alarmed, Mamma.

The STRANGER *deposits* MARIANNE *on the sofa. They look straight into each other's eyes. Electric.*

>   THE STRANGER
>   I can assure you it is not serious. I took the liberty of feeling the
>   bone and it is perfectly sound.

ELINOR *raises her eyebrows at* MARIANNE, *who blushes to her roots.*

>   MRS DASHWOOD
>   Sir, I cannot even begin to thank you.

>   THE STRANGER
>   Please do not think of it. I am honoured to be of service.

>   MRS DASHWOOD
>   Will you not be seated?

>   THE STRANGER
>   Pray excuse me – I have no desire to leave a water mark! But
>   permit me to call tomorrow afternoon and enquire after the
>   patient?

>   MRS DASHWOOD
>   We shall look forward to it!

He turns to MARIANNE *and smiles. She smiles back gloriously. He bows, and sweeps out of the room.*

MARIANNE (*hissing*)
His name! His name!

MRS DASHWOOD *silences her with a gesture and follows him out with all
the solicitous charm she can command while* MARGARET *pokes her head
around the door to watch.* ELINOR *is removing* MARIANNE's *boot and
trying not to laugh at her.*

63 EXT. BARTON COTTAGE. FRONT DOOR. DAY.
MRS DASHWOOD *calls out after him.*

MRS DASHWOOD
Please tell us to whom we are so much obliged?

The STRANGER *mounts Bedivere and turns to her.*

THE STRANGER
John Willoughby of Allenham – your servant, ma'am!

And he gallops off into the mist – we almost expect Bedivere to sprout wings.
CLOSE *on* MRS DASHWOOD's *excited expression.*

64 INT. BARTON COTTAGE. PARLOUR. DAY.
MRS DASHWOOD *runs back into the parlour, jittering with excitement and
anxiety.*

MARIANNE
Mr John Willoughby of Allenham!

MRS DASHWOOD
What an impressive gentleman!

MARIANNE
He lifted me as if I weighed no more than a dried leaf!

ELINOR
Is he human?

MARIANNE *hits* ELINOR. MRS DASHWOOD *tends to her ankle.*

MRS DASHWOOD
Tell me if I hurt you.

ELINOR (*regarding Marianne's ecstatic expression*)
She feels no pain, Mamma. Margaret, ask Betsy to make up a cold compress, please.

MARGARET (*leaving reluctantly*)
Did you see him? He expressed himself well, did he not?

MRS DASHWOOD
With great decorum and honour.

MARIANNE
And spirit and wit and feeling.

ELINOR
And economy -- ten words at most.

From below stairs we can hear MARGARET *wailing*

Wait for me!

MARIANNE
And he is to come tomorrow!

ELINOR
You must change, Marianne – you will catch a cold.

MARIANNE
What care I for colds when there is such a man?

ELINOR
You will care very much when your nose swells up.

MARIANNE
You are right. Help me, Elinor.

MARGARET *comes back with the bandages.*

MARGARET
What has happened?

ELINOR
We have decided to give you to the Gypsies.

ELINOR *and* MARGARET *go upstairs.* MARGARET *whispers to* MRS
DASHWOOD.

MARGARET
Will they be married before Edward and Elinor, do you think,
Mamma?

MRS DASHWOOD
Margaret, you are worse than Mrs Jennings.

65 EXT. BARTON COTTAGE. MORNING.

The rain has cleared. SIR JOHN's horse munches grass contentedly by the side of the road.

> SIR JOHN (V/O)
> Mr Willoughby is well worth catching, Miss Dashwood – Miss Marianne must not expect to have all the men to herself!

66 INT. BARTON COTTAGE. PARLOUR. MORNING.

The DASHWOODS are having a frustrating time winkling information about WILLOUGHBY out of SIR JOHN, who is in turn only anxious to protect BRANDON's interest. MARIANNE has her bandaged foot up on the sofa and is fast losing patience.

> MARIANNE
> But what do you know of Mr Willoughby, Sir John?

> SIR JOHN
> Decent shot – and there is not a bolder rider in all England.

> MARIANNE
> But what is he *like*?

> SIR JOHN
> Like?

> MARIANNE
> What are his tastes? His passions? His pursuits?

> SIR JOHN (*mystified*)
> Well, he has the nicest little bitch of a pointer – was she out with him yesterday?

MARIANNE gives up. MRS DASHWOOD takes over.

> MRS DASHWOOD
> Where is Allenham, Sir John?

SIR JOHN

Nice little estate three miles east. He is to inherit it from an elderly relative – Lady Allen is her name.

Now they are getting somewhere. MARIANNE is about to ask another question when they hear a horse galloping up. Everyone is electrified. MARGARET runs to the window and turns back in disappointment.

MARGARET

It is Colonel Brandon. I shall go outside and keep watch.

MARGARET runs out of the room.

SIR JOHN

You are all on the lookout for Willoughby, eh? Dear me, poor Brandon. You will none of you think of him now.

BRANDON is admitted by BETSY. He is carrying a large bunch of hothouse flowers.

COLONEL BRANDON

How is the invalid?

He hands MARIANNE the flowers with a smile.

MARIANNE

Thank you so much, Colonel.

She rather absently hands the flowers to ELINOR, who goes for a vase. SIR JOHN gestures at BRANDON with bluff insensitivity.

SIR JOHN

Miss Marianne, I cannot see why you should set your cap at Mr Willoughby when you have already made such a splendid conquest!

MARIANNE

I have no intention of 'setting my cap' at anyone, Sir John!

COLONEL BRANDON
Mr Willoughby – Lady Allen's nephew?

BRANDON's light tone betrays no emotion. ELINOR comes back in with the flowers and puts them on the table next to MARIANNE.

SIR JOHN
Aye, he visits every year for he is to inherit Allenham – and he has a very pretty estate of his own, Miss Dashwood, Combe Magna in Somerset. If I were you, I would not give him up to my younger sister in spite of all this tumbling down hills . . .

Suddenly MARGARET runs in screaming 'Marianne's preserver!' at the top of her voice. Everyone starts to move at once. MARGARET is silenced. BRANDON looks at MARIANNE, whose incandescent expression makes her feelings all too clear.

SIR JOHN
Here is the man himself. Come, Brandon – we know when we are not wanted. Let us leave him to the ladies!

ELINOR
Marianne! Sir John and the Colonel are leaving.

MARIANNE looks up, suddenly self-conscious.

MARIANNE
Goodbye, Colonel. Thank you for the flowers.

ELINOR sees them out. We hear WILLOUGHBY's voice outside. CLOSE on MARIANNE's radiant anticipation.

67 EXT. BARTON COTTAGE. FRONT DOOR. DAY.
WILLOUGHBY *is shaking hands with* COLONEL BRANDON *and* SIR JOHN.

WILLOUGHBY
How do you do, Colonel?

SIR JOHN

How does *he* do? How do *you* do, more like. Go on in, they're waiting for you!

BRANDON *looks at* WILLOUGHBY *for a moment. He bows.* WILLOUGHBY *bows. Then* BRANDON *and* SIR JOHN *exit.*

68 INT. BARTON COTTAGE. PARLOUR. DAY.
ELINOR *leads in* WILLOUGHBY. MRS DASHWOOD *greets him with outstretched arms.*

MRS DASHWOOD

Mr Willoughby! What a pleasure to see you again!

WILLOUGHBY

The pleasure is all mine, I can assure you. I trust Miss Marianne has not caught cold?

MARIANNE
You have found out my name!

WILLOUGHBY
Of course. The neighbourhood is crawling with my spies.

He suddenly produces a bunch of wild flowers from behind his back and offers them to MARIANNE *with a courtly, humorous bow.*

WILLOUGHBY
And since you cannot venture out to nature, nature must be brought to you!

MARIANNE
How beautiful. *These* are not from the hothouse.

WILLOUGHBY *sees* BRANDON's *flowers.*

WILLOUGHBY
Ah! I see mine is not the first offering, nor the most elegant. I am afraid I obtained these from an obliging field.

MARIANNE
But I have always preferred wild flowers!

WILLOUGHBY
I suspected as much.

ELINOR *takes the delicate flowers from* WILLOUGHBY.

ELINOR
I will put these in water.

MRS DASHWOOD
Our gratitude, Mr Willoughby, is beyond expression –

WILLOUGHBY
But it is I who am grateful. I have often passed this cottage and grieved for its lonely state – and then the first news I had from

Lady Allen when I arrived was that it was taken. I felt a peculiar interest in the event which nothing can account for but my present delight in meeting you.

He is merry, spirited, voluble – a breath of fresh air. ELINOR *brings back* WILLOUGHBY's *flowers and places them next to* BRANDON's *on the side table.*

MRS DASHWOOD
Pray sit down, Mr Willoughby.

She indicates a chair but WILLOUGHBY *sees a book lying on* MAR-IANNE's *footstool, picks it up and – to her great delight – sits down on the stool at her feet.*

WILLOUGHBY
Who is reading Shakespeare's sonnets?

Everyone answers at once.

MARIANNE/ELINOR/MRS DASHWOOD
I am. / We all are. / Marianne.

MRS DASHWOOD
Marianne has been reading them out to us.

WILLOUGHBY
Which are your favourites?

It is a general question but MARIANNE *gaily commandeers it.*

MARIANNE
Without a doubt, mine is 116.

WILLOUGHBY
Let me not to the marriage of true minds
Admit impediments. Love is not love
Which alters when it alteration finds,
Or bends with the remover to remove –
then how does it go?

———

97

MARIANNE

'O, no! it is an ever-fixed mark.'

WILLOUGHBY *joins in the line halfway through and continues.* ELINOR *and* MRS DASHWOOD *exchange glances. Clearly, their contribution to this conversation will be minimal.*

WILLOUGHBY

'That looks on storms' – or is it tempests? Let me find it.

WILLOUGHBY *gets out a tiny leatherbound book.*

WILLOUGHBY

It is strange you should be reading them – for, look, I carry this with me always.

It is a miniature copy of the sonnets. MARIANNE *is delighted, and, mutually astonished at this piece of synchronicity, they proceed to look up other favourites, chatting as though they were already intimates.* MRS DASH-WOOD *smiles at* ELINOR *with satisfaction.* ELINOR, *amused, picks up her sewing.* MARGARET *stares.* WILLOUGHBY *and* MARIANNE *are oblivious to everything but each other.*

69 EXT. BARTON COTTAGE. GARDEN PATH. DAY.
WILLOUGHBY *is leaving. He has a flower from* MARIANNE's *bunch in his buttonhole and is on his horse, looking about as virile as his horse. Everyone has come out to say goodbye,* MARIANNE *supported by* ELINOR *and* MRS DASHWOOD.

WILLOUGHBY

Till tomorrow! And my pocket sonnets are yours, Miss Marianne! A talisman against further injury!

MARIANNE

Goodbye! Thank you!

He gallops off. They all wave. MARGARET *follows him down the road for a while.*

ELINOR

Good work, Marianne! You have covered all forms of poetry; another meeting will ascertain his views on nature and romantic attachments and then you will have nothing left to talk about and the acquaintanceship will be over.

MARIANNE

I suppose I have erred against decorum. I should have been dull and spiritless and talked only of the weather, or the state of the roads . . .

ELINOR

No, but Mr Willoughby can be in no doubt of your enthusiasm for him.

MARIANNE

Why should he doubt it? Why should I hide my regard?

ELINOR

No particular reason, Marianne, only that we know so little of him –

MARIANNE

But time alone does not determine intimacy. Seven years would be insufficient to make some people acquainted with each other and seven days are more than enough for others.

ELINOR

Or seven hours in this case.

MARIANNE

I feel I know Mr Willoughby well already. If I had weaker, more shallow feelings perhaps I *could* conceal them, as you do –

Then she realises what she's said.

MRS DASHWOOD
Marianne, that is not fair –

MARIANNE
I am sorry, Elinor, I did not mean . . .

ELINOR
I know. Do not trouble yourself, Marianne.

ELINOR *turns back into the house.*

MARIANNE
I do not understand her, Mamma. Why does she never mention Edward? I have never even seen her cry about him, or about Norland . . .

MRS DASHWOOD
Nor I. But Elinor is not like you or I, dear. She does not like to be swayed by her emotions.

70 INT. BARTON COTTAGE. ELINOR AND MARIANNE'S BEDROOM. DAY.
CLOSE *on Edward's handkerchief. We can see the monogram ECF clearly.* CLOSE *on* ELINOR *staring out of the window. Tears stand in her eyes but she presses the handkerchief to them before they fall.*

71 INT. BARTON PARK. DRAWING ROOM. EVE.
After dinner. Tea has been served. ELINOR, COLONEL BRANDON, MRS DASHWOOD *and* MRS JENNINGS *play at cards. In a far corner of the room,* MARIANNE *is concentrating as she draws a silhouette.* WILLOUGH-BY's *profile glows behind the screen in front of her. She looks up and stops, gazing, bewitched, at his beauty. The lips move – a whisper:* Marianne. *Then, louder:* Haven't you finished? *He moves out from behind the screen, eyes full of laughter. They look at each other.*

73A INT. BARTON COTTAGE. PARLOUR. DAY.
ELINOR *and* MRS DASHWOOD *are at the accounts.* WILLOUGHBY *and*

MARIANNE *are on the other side of the room in the window seat, whispering together. Clearly, he is already part of the family.*

MRS DASHWOOD

Surely you are not going to deny us beef as well as sugar?

ELINOR

There is nothing under tenpence a pound. We have to economise.

MRS DASHWOOD

Do you want us to starve?

ELINOR

No. Just not to eat beef.

MRS DASHWOOD *is silenced but sighs crossly.* ELINOR *looks over to the lovers and sees* WILLOUGHBY *in the act of cutting off a lock of MAR-IANNE's hair, which he kisses and places in his pocket-book.* ELINOR *is transfixed by this strangely erotic moment.* WILLOUGHBY *senses her gaze and looks over. She snaps her head back to her sums and is astonished to find that she has written 'Edward' at the top of the sheet. Hastily she rubs it out and writes 'Expenses'.*

73B EXT. BARTON CHURCH. DAY.
MRS JENNINGS *is talking to the elderly* CURATE. *Other* PARISHIONERS *exit the church as* WILLOUGHBY's *curricle (the eighteenth-century equivalent of a sports car) goes flying by.* MARIANNE *sits by his side, the picture of happiness.* MRS JENNINGS *nudges the* CURATE *and whispers. The* PARISHIONERS *stare after them and comment to each other.*

74 EXT. BARTON COTTAGE. GARDEN PATH. DAY.
MARIANNE *and* ELINOR *are coming down the path together.* MAR-IANNE *is dressed to go out. The argument has evidently started indoors and is being continued here.*

MARIANNE
If there was any *true* impropriety in my behaviour, I should be sensible of it, Elinor –

ELINOR
But as it has already exposed you to some very impertinent remarks, do you not begin to doubt your own discretion?

MARIANNE
If the impertinent remarks of such as Mrs Jennings are proof of impropriety, then we are all offending every moment of our lives –

The conversation is halted by the arrival of COLONEL BRANDON *on horseback.*

COLONEL BRANDON (*dismounting*)
Miss Dashwood! Miss Marianne!

ELINOR

Good morning, Colonel!

COLONEL BRANDON

I come to issue an invitation. A picnic on my estate at Delaford – if you would care to join us on Thursday next. Mrs Jennings's daughter and her husband are travelling up especially.

ELINOR

Thank you, Colonel, we shall be delighted.

At that moment, WILLOUGHBY's *curricle hoves into view and* MAR-IANNE's *face lights up.*

COLONEL BRANDON (*to Marianne*)

I will of course be including Mr Willoughby in the party.

Even MARIANNE *is a little embarrassed and recollects her manners. She smiles kindly at* BRANDON.

MARIANNE

I should be delighted to join you, Colonel!

The COLONEL *helps her into the curricle, exchanging nods with* WIL-LOUGHBY, *who is regarding him with some suspicion.*

WILLOUGHBY

Good morning, Miss Dashwood; good morning, Colonel.

MARIANNE

The Colonel has invited us to Delaford, Willoughby!

WILLOUGHBY

Excellent. I understand you have a particularly fine pianoforte, Colonel.

The undercurrents of this conversation are decidedly tense.

COLONEL BRANDON
A Broadwood Grand.

MARIANNE
A Broadwood Grand! Then I shall really be able to play for you!

WILLOUGHBY
We shall look forward to it!

MARIANNE *smiles her perfect happiness at him and he whips up the horses. They drive off, waving their farewells.*

BRANDON *looks after them for a silent moment, and then collects himself and turns to* ELINOR, *who is less than satisfied with their behaviour.*

COLONEL BRANDON
Your sister seems very happy.

ELINOR
Yes. Marianne does not approve of hiding her emotions. In fact, her romantic prejudices have the unfortunate tendency to set propriety at naught.

COLONEL BRANDON
She is wholly unspoilt.

ELINOR
Rather too unspoilt, in my view. The sooner she becomes acquainted with the ways of the world, the better.

COLONEL BRANDON *looks at her sharply and then speaks very deliberately, as though controlling some powerful emotion.*

COLONEL BRANDON
I knew a lady like your sister – the same impulsive sweetness of temper – who was forced into, as you put it, a better acquaintance with the world. The result was only ruination and despair.

He stops, and briskly remounts his horse.

> COLONEL BRANDON
> Do not desire it, Miss Dashwood.

75 EXT. BARTON PARK. DRIVE. DAY.
People and carriages fill the drive, the sun shines and the atmosphere is pleasantly expectant. SIR JOHN is organising the provision of blankets and parasols and COLONEL BRANDON is busy furnishing the DRIVERS with their routes. There are three new faces a pretty, blowsy WOMAN (CHARLOTTE PALMER), a stony-faced MAN (MR PALMER) and an exceedingly good-looking GIRL (LUCY STEELE), who are standing with ELINOR, MARIANNE, MARGARET, MRS JENNINGS and MRS DASH-WOOD.

MARIANNE is standing slightly apart, looking out along the road, impatient for WILLOUGHBY.

> MRS JENNINGS
> Imagine my surprise, Mrs Dashwood, when Charlotte and her lord and master appeared with our cousin Lucy! The last person I expected to see! 'Where did you pop out from, Miss?' says I. I was never so surprised to see anyone in all my life!

LUCY STEELE smiles shyly and looks at the ground. MRS JENNINGS continues sotto voce *to MRS DASHWOOD.*

> MRS JENNINGS
> She probably came on purpose to share the fun, for there are no funds for such luxuries at home, poor thing.

> LUCY
> I had not seen you for so long, dear Mrs Jennings, I could not resist the opportunity.

> CHARLOTTE
> Oh, you sly thing! It was the Misses Dashwood she wanted to

---

see, not Delaford, Mamma! I have heard nothing but 'Miss Dashwood this, Miss Dashwood that' for I don't know how long! And what do you think of them now you do see them, Lucy? My mother has talked of nothing else in her letters since you came to Barton, Mrs Dashwood. Mr Palmer – are they not the very creatures she describes?

MR PALMER *regards his wife with a less than enchanted expression.*

MR PALMER

Nothing like.

CHARLOTTE (laughing gaily)

Why, Mr Palmer! Do you know you are quite rude today? He is to be an MP, you know, Mrs Dashwood, and it is very fatiguing for him for he is forced to make everybody like him – he says it is quite shocking –

MRS PALMER

I never said anything so irrational. Don't palm all your abuses of the language upon me.

MRS JENNINGS (to Mrs Dashwood)

Mr Palmer is so droll – he is always out of humour.

MR PALMER *does indeed have the air of a man under siege.* WILLOUGH-BY *suddenly appears in his curricle.* MARIANNE *waves to him with a radiant smile.* MRS JENNINGS *nudges* CHARLOTTE *and points to* MARIANNE.

MRS JENNINGS

Here he is! Now you shall see, Charlotte.

WILLOUGHBY *drives up as close to* MARIANNE *as possible, making her laugh.*

MRS JENNINGS

How now, Mr Willoughby! You must greet my daughter Charlotte, and Mr Palmer –

WILLOUGHBY

How do you do?

MRS JENNINGS

And my little cousin, Miss Lucy Steele.

WILLOUGHBY

Welcome to our party, Miss Steele!

LUCY *bobs demurely.* WILLOUGHBY *inclines his head politely, leaps from the curricle and hands* MARIANNE *in.* MRS JENNINGS *coos and chuckles at them.* CHARLOTTE *nudges* ELINOR.

CHARLOTTE

I know Mr Willoughby extremely well – not that I ever spoke to him but I have seen him forever in town. Your sister is monstrous lucky to get him. Mamma says Colonel Brandon is in love with her as well, which is a very great compliment for he hardly ever falls in love with anyone.

ELINOR *smiles politely.* WILLOUGHBY *moves the curricle out to the front of the drive.* CHARLOTTE *points after them and laughs with* MRS JENNINGS. LUCY *edges up beside* ELINOR.

LUCY

May I beg a seat beside you, Miss Dashwood? I have so longed to make your better acquaintance! I have heard nothing but the highest praise for you.

ELINOR *is relieved to change the subject.*

ELINOR

I would be delighted. But Sir John and Mrs Jennings are too excessive in their compliments. I am sure to disappoint.

———

LUCY

No, for it was from quite another source that I heard you praised and one not at all inclined to exaggeration.

LUCY *speaks in a knowing, confidential undertone, as though not wanting anyone else to hear. At that moment a* HORSEMAN *thunders up the drive towards them. Everyone turns to face the new arrival.*

SIR JOHN

What can this be?

It is a MESSENGER *who has obviously had a long, hard ride. He asks for* COLONEL BRANDON *and hands him a letter, which* BRANDON *tears open.* MRS JENNINGS *is puce with suppressed curiosity.*

COLONEL BRANDON

My horse! Quickly!

SIR JOHN

What is the matter, Brandon?

COLONEL BRANDON

I must away to London.

SIR JOHN

No! Impossible!

Everyone gathers round BRANDON, *who is, naturally, mortified. A* SERVANT *brings up the* COLONEL's *horse.*

COLONEL BRANDON

Imperative.

There is a murmur of disappointment from the party. SIR JOHN *is embarrassed and protests again.*

SIR JOHN

But Brandon, we are all assembled. We cannot picnic at Delaford without our host! Go up to town tomorrow.

WILLOUGHBY

Or wait till we return and start then – you would not be six hours later.

COLONEL BRANDON

I cannot afford to lose one minute.

As he speaks, he is mounting his horse. His grave urgency silences all protest and he gallops off, leaving everyone stunned and, of course, deeply curious. Then they all start to talk at once. LUCY is still next to ELINOR.

LUCY

Oh, Miss Dashwood, I cannot bear it! Just when I was to have the opportunity of speaking with you.

76 EXT. MEADOW NEAR BARTON COTTAGE. DAY.
Having been denied their trip, the DASHWOODS and WILLOUGHBY have set out an impromptu picnic. WILLOUGHBY is wandering restlessly about. The weather is sublime.

WILLOUGHBY

Frailty, thy name is Brandon!

MARIANNE

There are some people who cannot bear a party of pleasure. I think he wrote the letter himself as a trick for getting out of it.

MRS DASHWOOD (*indulgently*)

You are a very wicked pair, Colonel Brandon will be sadly missed.

WILLOUGHBY

Why? When he is the kind of man that everyone speaks well of and no one wants to talk to.

MARIANNE

Exactly!

———

ELINOR

Nonsense.

MRS DASHWOOD

Colonel Brandon is very highly esteemed at the Park.

WILLOUGHBY

Which is enough censure in itself.

ELINOR (*half laughing*)

Really, Willoughby!

WILLOUGHBY (*imitating Mrs Jennings perfectly*)

Come, come, Mr Impudence – I know you and your wicked ways – oh!

He gives a little shriek and waddles about the garden doing her walk. He comes up to ELINOR *and puts his head on her shoulder.*

WILLOUGHBY

Come, Miss Dashwood, reveal your beau, reveal him, I say! Let's have no secrets between friends! Let me winkle them out of you!

ELINOR *hits him on the nose with her teaspoon and he waddles off to* MARIANNE.

WILLOUGHBY (*as Mrs Jennings*)

I declare, Miss Marianne, if I do not have you married to the Colonel by teatime, I shall swallow my own bonnet.

MARIANNE *laughs.* WILLOUGHBY *drops the parody suddenly.*

WILLOUGHBY

As if you *could* marry such a character.

ELINOR

Why should you dislike him?

———

There is indeed an edge to WILLOUGHBY's *raillery. He flicks* ELINOR *an almost alarmed glance and then sweeps* MARIANNE *to her feet and starts to dance around the garden with her.*

WILLOUGHBY

Because he has threatened me with rain when I wanted it fine, he has found fault with the balance of my curricle and I cannot persuade him to buy my brown mare. If it will be of any satisfaction to you, however, to be told I believe his character to be in all other respects irreproachable, I am ready to confess it. And in return for an acknowledgement that must give me some pain (*he is slowing down*) you cannot deny me the privilege (*slower still*) of disliking *him* (*and stopping*) as much as I *adore* —

He and MARIANNE *are standing looking at each other. The expression on* WILLOUGHBY's *face is heart-stopping.* MARGARET *has stopped eating and is staring with her mouth open.*

ELINOR *glances at* MRS DASHWOOD *but she is gazing up at them with almost as many stars in her eyes as* MARIANNE.

Suddenly WILLOUGHBY *breaks the mood by swinging away from* MARIANNE *and gesturing to the house.*

WILLOUGHBY

– this cottage!

The tension is broken. MARGARET *starts to chew again.*

MRS DASHWOOD

I have great plans for improvements to it, you know, Mr Willoughby.

WILLOUGHBY

Now *that* I will never consent to. Not a stone must be added to its walls. Were I rich enough, I would instantly pull down Combe

113

Magna and build it up again in the exact image of that cottage!

ELINOR

With dark, narrow stairs, a poky hall and a fire that smokes?

WILLOUGHBY

Especially the fire that smokes! Then I might be as happy at Combe Magna as I have been at Barton.

He looks at MARIANNE, *who has gone to sit at her mother's feet.*

WILLOUGHBY

But this place has one claim on my affection which no other can possibly share.

MARIANNE *is so irradiated with happiness that she looks like an angel.*

WILLOUGHBY

Promise me you will never change it.

MRS DASHWOOD

I do not have the heart.

ELINOR

Or the money.

77 EXT. BARTON COTTAGE. GARDEN PATH AND GATE. DUSK.
MARIANNE *is seeing* WILLOUGHBY *off.*

WILLOUGHBY

Miss Marianne, will you – will you do me the honour of granting me an interview tomorrow – alone?

MARIANNE

Willoughby, we are always alone!

WILLOUGHBY

But there is something very particular I should like to ask you.

There is something about his formal tone that makes her feel shy.

———

MARIANNE

Of course. I shall ask Mamma if I may stay behind from church.

WILLOUGHBY

Thank you. Until tomorrow then – Miss Marianne.

He mounts Bedivere and leaves. MARIANNE looks after him, her eyes shining. He is coming to propose.

78 EXT. LONDON TENEMENTS. NIGHT.

A district of extreme poverty, populated by the LOWLIFE *of* LONDON: FOOTPADS, *dogs, rats and* SCAVENGERS *of all kinds. In the distance a tavern belches forth drunken* REVELLERS *who sway and reel into the night. A hooded* HORSEMAN *pulls up his exhausted steed at the entrance to a slum. He dismounts and looks up at one of the windows. The rags hanging there twitch as if someone is watching for him. He strides inside.*

79 INT. TENEMENT STAIRS. NIGHT.

Stepping over a supine BEGGAR *at the foot of the stairs, the* HORSEMAN *flings back his hood – it is* BRANDON, *hollow-eyed and dropping with weariness. We follow him up the stairs to a door which is opened by an* OLDER WOMAN.

80 INT. TENEMENT ROOM. NIGHT.

He enters a bare room partitioned with filthy rags hung from the ceiling and lit with stinking tallow lamps. At the window stands the slight figure of a VERY YOUNG WOMAN. *She turns.* BRANDON *reacts with a tender smile which stiffens into an expression of deep shock. We see her silhouette. She is heavily pregnant. She bursts into tears and runs into his arms.*

81 INT. BARTON CHURCH. DAY.

Amongst the small CONGREGATION *listening to the sermon drone on, we see the excited faces of* ELINOR, MARGARET *and* MRS DASHWOOD.

MARGARET

Do you think he will kneel down when he asks her?

115

ELINOR

Shhh!

MARGARET (*with satisfaction*)
They always kneel down.

82 EXT. BARTON COTTAGE. GARDEN PATH. DAY.
The DASHWOODS *return from church to find* THOMAS *grooming Bedivere at the garden gate. Their excitement mounts.*

83 INT. BARTON COTTAGE. FRONT DOOR. DAY.
They all enter the cottage, talking nonsense loudly in order to signal their presence. MARGARET *giggles. Suddenly,* MARIANNE *bursts out of the parlour sobbing, and disappears into the room opposite.* ELINOR *and* MARGARET *stand by the door in utter consternation, while* MRS DASH-WOOD *goes to* MARIANNE.

116

MRS DASHWOOD
What is wrong, my dearest?

MARIANNE *shakes her head and waves them away.*

84 INT. BARTON COTTAGE. PARLOUR. DAY.
ELINOR, MARGARET *and* MRS DASHWOOD *enter to find* WIL-
LOUGHBY *standing in a frozen attitude by the fireplace.*

MRS DASHWOOD
Willoughby! What is the matter?

WILLOUGHBY
I – forgive me, Mrs Dashwood. I am sent – that is to say, Lady
Allen has exercised the privilege of riches upon a dependent
cousin and is sending me to London.

He cannot look any of them in the eye.

MRS DASHWOOD
When – this morning?

WILLOUGHBY
Almost this moment.

MRS DASHWOOD
How very disappointing! But your business will not detain you
from us for long, I hope?

WILLOUGHBY
You are very kind – but I have no idea of returning immediately
to Devonshire. I am seldom invited to Allenham more than once
a year.

MRS DASHWOOD
For shame, Willoughby! Can you wait for an invitation from
Barton Cottage?

———

WILLOUGHBY
My engagements at present are of such a nature – that is – I dare
not flatter myself –

The atmosphere is thick with tension. WILLOUGHBY *flicks a glance at the*
three WOMEN *staring at him in mute astonishment.*

WILLOUGHBY
It is folly to linger in this manner. I will not torment myself
further.

He rushes past them and out of the cottage. They follow him to the door.

85 EXT. BARTON COTTAGE. FRONT DOOR. DAY.
The DASHWOODS *cluster round the door.*

MARGARET
Willoughby, come back!

She is silenced by ELINOR *as* WILLOUGHBY *seizes Bedivere's reins from*
THOMAS, *mounts up and rides off at a furious pace.*

86 INT. BARTON COTTAGE. PARLOUR. DAY.
They all rush back into the parlour.

ELINOR
Meg, dearest, please ask Betsy to make a cup of hot tea for
Marianne.

MARGARET *nods dumbly and goes.* MRS DASHWOOD *has her arms*
around MARIANNE.

MRS DASHWOOD
What is wrong, my love?

MARIANNE
Nothing! Please do not ask me questions!

MARIANNE *struggles free.*

118

MARIANNE

Please let me be!

She runs off upstairs and we hear her bedroom door slamming. There is a moment of stunned silence.

ELINOR

They must have quarrelled.

MRS DASHWOOD

That is unlikely. Perhaps this – Lady Allen – disapproves of his regard for Marianne and has invented an excuse to send him away?

ELINOR

Then why did he not say as much? It is not like Willoughby to be secretive. Did he think Marianne was richer than she is?

MRS DASHWOOD

How could he?

She gestures to the room and then looks at ELINOR *with a frown.*

MRS DASHWOOD

What is it you suspect him of?

ELINOR

I can hardly tell you. But why was his manner so guilty?

MRS DASHWOOD

What are you saying, Elinor? That he has been acting a part to your sister for all this time?

MRS DASHWOOD *is getting defensive.* ELINOR *pauses to think.*

ELINOR

No, he loves her, I am sure.

MRS DASHWOOD
Of course he loves her!

ELINOR
But has he left her with any assurance of his return? Cannot you ask her if he has proposed?

MRS DASHWOOD
Certainly not. I cannot force a confidence from Marianne and nor must you. We must trust her to confide in us in her own time.

ELINOR (*shaking her head*)
There was something so underhand in the manner of his leaving.

MRS DASHWOOD
You are resolved, then, to think the worst of him.

ELINOR
Not resolved –

MRS DASHWOOD (*cold*)
I prefer to give him the benefit of my good opinion. He deserves no less. From all of us.

She stalks out of the room and starts up the stairs. ELINOR *follows her.*

ELINOR
Mamma, I am very fond of Willoughby –

MRS DASHWOOD *goes into her bedroom and shuts the door.* ELINOR *is halfway up the stairs. She meets a wet-eyed* MARGARET *coming down with a cup of tea.*

MARGARET
She would not let me in.

ELINOR *takes the cup and* MARGARET *runs out into the garden in tears.*

———

The sound of sobbing also comes from MARIANNE's *room, and now from* MRS DASHWOOD's *as well.* ELINOR *sits down helplessly on the stairs and drinks the tea.*

87 EXT. BARTON COTTAGE. RAIN. DAY.
The rain has settled in. The cottage looks cold and bleak.

88 INT. BARTON COTTAGE. UPSTAIRS CORRIDOR. DAY.
BETSY *carries another uneaten meal from* MARIANNE's *room. She looks at the food and tuts in anxiety.*

89 INT. BARTON COTTAGE. ELINOR AND MARIANNE'S BEDROOM. DAY.
MARIANNE *is sitting by the window looking out at the rain through tear-swollen eyes.* WILLOUGHBY's *sonnets are on her lap.*

> MARIANNE
> How like a winter hath my absence been
> From thee, the pleasure of the fleeting year!
> What freezings have I felt, what dark days seen!
> What old December's bareness everywhere!

91 EXT. BARTON PARK. RAIN. EVE.
Smoke issues from every chimney in the place.

92 INT. BARTON PARK. DRAWING ROOM. EVE.
Dinner is over. MARIANNE *sits listlessly by the window.* MR PALMER *is hiding behind a newspaper.* SIR JOHN *and* MARGARET *are looking at a map and discussing routes through China.* LUCY, CHARLOTTE, MRS DASHWOOD *and* MRS JENNINGS *are at cards.* ELINOR *is reading.*

> CHARLOTTE
> Oh! If only this rain would stop!

> MR PALMER (*from behind the paper*)
> If only *you* would stop.

MRS JENNINGS *and* CHARLOTTE *laugh at him.*

MRS JENNINGS

'Twas you took her off my hands, Mr Palmer, and a very good bargain you made of it too, but now I have the whip hand over you for you cannot give her back!

The heavy silence behind the paper attests to the unhappy truth of this statement.

MRS JENNINGS

Miss Marianne, come and play a round with us! Looking out at the weather will not bring him back.

CHARLOTTE (*sotto voce*)

She ate nothing at dinner.

MRS JENNINGS

Mind, we are all a little forlorn these days. London has swallowed all our company.

CHARLOTTE *and* MRS JENNINGS *start to gossip about the disappearances of* BRANDON *and* WILLOUGHBY. LUCY *walks over and sits by* ELINOR, *who politely puts aside the book.*

LUCY (*low*)

Dear Miss Dashwood, perhaps now we might have our – discussion . . .

ELINOR

Our discussion?

LUCY *looks around at* MRS JENNINGS *and lowers her voice still further, so that* ELINOR *is obliged to move her chair nearer.*

LUCY

There is a particular question I have long wanted to ask you, but perhaps you will think me impertinent?

ELINOR

I cannot imagine so.

LUCY

But it is an odd question. Forgive me, I have no wish to trouble you –

She looks away coyly as if deciding whether to speak.

ELINOR

My dear Miss Steele –

CHARLOTTE (*interrupting*)

Miss Dashwood, if only Mr Willoughby had gone home to Combe Magna, we could have taken Miss Marianne to see him! For we live but half a mile away.

———

MR PALMER

Five and a half.

CHARLOTTE

No, I cannot believe it is that far, for you can see the place from
the top of our hill. Is it really five and a half miles? No! I cannot
believe it.

MR PALMER

Try.

ELINOR

You have my permission to ask any manner of question, if that
is of any help.

LUCY

Thank you. I wonder, are you at all acquainted with your sister-
in-law's mother? Mrs Ferrars?

ELINOR *sits back in deep surprise.*

ELINOR

With Fanny's mother? No, I have never met her.

LUCY

I am sure you think me strange for enquiring – if I dared tell –

MRS JENNINGS (*shouting over*)

If she tells you aught of the famous 'Mr F', Lucy, you are to
pass it on.

ELINOR *tries to ignore* MRS JENNINGS, *who is keeping a curious eye on
them.*

LUCY

Will you take a turn with me, Miss Dashwood?

LUCY *rises and takes* ELINOR's *arm. She guides her as far away as possible
from* MRS JENNINGS *and* CHARLOTTE.

———

ELINOR

I had no idea at all that you were connected with that family.

LUCY

Oh! I am certainly nothing to Mrs Ferrars at present – but the time may come when we may be very *intimately* connected.

ELINOR (*low*)

What do you mean? Do you have an understanding with Fanny's brother Robert?

LUCY

The youngest? No, I never saw him in my life. No, with Edward.

ELINOR

Edward?

ELINOR *stops walking.*

ELINOR

Edward Ferrars?

LUCY *nods.*

LUCY

Edward and I have been secretly engaged these five years.

ELINOR *is frozen to the spot.*

LUCY

You may well be surprised. I should never have mentioned it, had I not known I could entirely trust you to keep our secret. Edward cannot mind me telling you for he looks on you quite as his own sister.

ELINOR *walks on mechanically. Disbelief has set in.*

ELINOR

I am sorry, but we surely – we cannot mean the same Mr Ferrars?

———

LUCY

The very same – he was four years under the tutelage of my uncle Mr Pratt, down in Plymouth. Has he never spoken of it?

ELINOR (*awareness dawning*)
Mr Pratt! Yes, I believe he has . . .

LUCY

I was very unwilling to enter into it without his mother's approval but we loved each other with too great a passion for prudence. Though you do not know him so well as I, Miss Dashwood, you must have seen how capable he is of making a woman sincerely attached to him. I cannot pretend it has not been very hard on us both. We can hardly meet above twice a year.

She sniffs and produces a large handkerchief which she holds to her eyes so that the monogram is clearly visible. ECF. ELINOR, seeing the copy of the handkerchief she has held so dear, moves quickly to a chair and sits down.

LUCY

You seem out of sorts, Miss Dashwood – are you quite well?

ELINOR

Perfectly well, thank you.

LUCY

I have not offended you?

ELINOR

On the contrary.

MRS JENNINGS *has been watching. Now she rises, unable to contain herself.*

MRS JENNINGS

I can stand it no longer, I must know what you are saying, Lucy! Miss Dashwood is quite engrossed!

———

MRS JENNINGS *starts to bear down on them.* LUCY *whispers with real urgency.*

> LUCY
>
> Oh, Miss Dashwood, if anyone finds out, it will ruin him – you must not tell a soul! Edward says you would not break your word to save your life! Promise me!

ECU *on* ELINOR's *face.*

> ELINOR
>
> I give you my word.

MRS JENNINGS *looms over them.*

> MRS JENNINGS
>
> Well, what can have fascinated you to such an extent, Miss Dashwood?

> CHARLOTTE
>
> Tell us all!

ELINOR *cannot speak but* LUCY *glides smoothly in.*

> LUCY
>
> We were talking of London, ma'am, and all its – diversions.

> MRS JENNINGS
>
> Do you hear, Charlotte?

MRS JENNINGS *claps her hands delightedly.*

> MRS JENNINGS
>
> While you were so busy whispering, Charlotte and I have concocted a plan!

> CHARLOTTE
>
> It is the best plan in the world.

MRS JENNINGS

I make for London shortly and I invite you, Lucy, and both the Misses Dashwood to join me!

ELINOR *cannot hide her dismay.* MARIANNE *springs from her seat.*

MARIANNE

London!

MARGARET

Oh, can I go! Can *I* go?

MRS DASHWOOD

You know perfectly well you are too young, dearest.

MRS JENNINGS

I shall convey you all to my house in Berkeley Street and we shall taste all the delights of the season – what say you?

MARGARET

Oh, *please* can I go? I'm twelve soon.

CHARLOTTE

Mr Palmer, do you not long to have the Misses Dashwood come to London?

MR PALMER

I came into Devonshire with no other view.

ELINOR *exerts herself.*

ELINOR

Mrs Jennings, you are very kind, but we cannot possibly leave our mother . . .

LUCY'*s calculating eyes turn to* MRS DASHWOOD *with alacrity.*

LUCY

Indeed, the loss would be too great.

A chorus *of objections goes up, particularly from* MRS DASHWOOD, *who is both delighted and relieved to see* MARIANNE *with a smile on her face.*

MRS JENNINGS
Your mother can spare you very well.

MRS DASHWOOD
Of course I can!

CHARLOTTE
Of course she can!

SIR JOHN
And look at Miss Marianne – it would break her heart to deny her!

MRS JENNINGS
I will brook no refusal, Miss Dashwood!

MARIANNE *claps her hands, her eyes ablaze with joy.* MRS JENNINGS *takes* ELINOR's *hand.*

MRS JENNINGS
Let you and me strike hands upon the bargain – and if I do not have the three of you married by Michaelmas, it will not be my fault!

93 INT. BARTON COTTAGE. ELINOR/MARIANNE'S BEDROOM. NIGHT.
We are in ELINOR *and* MARIANNE's *bedroom.* ELINOR *is in bed. She is lying on her side with her back to* MARIANNE. *We are* CLOSE *on her face.* MARIANNE *is running around excitedly, pulling out ribbons, looking at dresses, etc.*

MARIANNE
I was never so grateful in all my life as I am to Mrs Jennings.

What a kind woman she is! I like her more than I can say. Oh,
Elinor! I shall see Willoughby. Think how surprised he will be!
And you will see Edward!

ELINOR *cannot reply.*

MARIANNE

Are you asleep?

ELINOR

With you in the room?

MARIANNE *laughs.*

MARIANNE

I do *not* believe you feel as calm as you look, not even you,
Elinor. I will never sleep tonight! Oh, what were you and Miss
Steele whispering about so long?

CLOSE *on* ELINOR's *expression as she struggles with the impossibility of
unburdening herself to her sister without breaking her promise to* LUCY.
After a pause –

ELINOR

Nothing of significance.

MARIANNE *looks at* ELINOR *curiously, then returns to her packing.*

95 EXT. BARTON COTTAGE. GARDEN GATE. DAY.
MRS DASHWOOD *and* MARGARET *are waving* MRS JENNINGS's
carriage off. MARIANNE *waves back with such exuberance that she
practically falls out.*

96 INT. MRS JENNINGS'S CARRIAGE. ROAD TO LONDON. DAY.
MRS JENNINGS *is chattering about London to* MARIANNE, *who listens
with new-found tolerance.* LUCY *is whispering into* ELINOR's *ear.*

LUCY

I have written to Edward, Miss Dashwood, and yet I do not

---

know how much I may see of him. Secrecy is vital – he will never be able to call.

                    ELINOR
I should imagine not.

                    LUCY
It is so hard. I believe my only comfort has been the constancy of his affection.

                    ELINOR
You are fortunate, over such a lengthy engagement, never to have had any doubts on that score.

LUCY *looks at* ELINOR *sharply, but* ELINOR *is impassive.*

                    LUCY
Oh! I am of rather a jealous nature and if he had talked more of one young lady than any other . . . but he has never given a moment's alarm on that count.

We can see from ELINOR'*s expression that she understands* LUCY *perfectly. The strain around her eyes is pronounced.*

                    LUCY
Imagine how glad he will be to learn that we are friends!

97A EXT. LONDON STREET. DAY.
MRS JENNINGS'*s carriage trundles along.*

98 EXT. MRS JENNINGS'S HOUSE. LONDON. DAY.
Establishing shot of a handsome town house. MRS JENNINGS'*s carriage comes into shot and stops in front of it.*

99 INT. MRS JENNINGS'S HOUSE. HALL. DAY.
They enter the grand hallway under the supercilious gaze of a powdered FOOTMAN (MR PIGEON). ELINOR *is haggard after two days of close proximity with* LUCY. MRS JENNINGS *is all officious bustle and* MAR-

---

IANNE *is feverish with anticipation. She whispers to* MRS JENNINGS, *who laughs heartily.*

MRS JENNINGS

To be sure, my dear, you must just hand it to Pigeon there. He will take care of it.

MARIANNE *hands a letter to the sphinxlike* FOOTMAN. *We can see a large W in the address.* ELINOR *looks at* MARIANNE *enquiringly but* MARIANNE *moves away from her.*

MRS JENNINGS

Lord above, you do not waste any time, Miss Marianne!

MARIANNE *glances self-consciously at* ELINOR *and follows* MRS JEN-NINGS *upstairs.* LUCY *goes up to* ELINOR *and whispers.*

LUCY

A letter! So they are definitely engaged! Mrs Jennings says your sister will buy her wedding clothes here in town.

ELINOR

Indeed Miss Steele, I know of no such plan.

But ELINOR *does not know what else to say. She marches firmly upstairs.*

100 INT. MRS JENNINGS'S HOUSE. DRAWING ROOM. DAY.
MARIANNE *and* ELINOR *have changed from their travelling clothes and are having a cup of tea. At least,* ELINOR *is.* MARIANNE *is pacing up and down in front of the window.*

ELINOR

John and Fanny are in town. I think we shall be forced to see them.

There is a faint knocking from somewhere. MARIANNE *jumps.*

ELINOR

I think it was for next door.

MARIANNE *looks out of the window.*

> MARIANNE
> Yes, you are right.

She sits down with a rueful smile. Suddenly a much louder rap is heard and they both jump. We hear a bustling downstairs. MARIANNE can hardly breathe. She goes to the drawing-room door, opens it, goes out, comes back in. We hear a MAN's voice.

> MARIANNE
> Oh, Elinor! It is Willoughby, indeed it is!

She turns and almost throws herself into the arms of COLONEL BRANDON.

> MARIANNE
> Oh! Excuse me, Colonel –

She leaves the room hastily. ELINOR is so ashamed of MARIANNE's rudeness that she does not at first notice BRANDON's mood of tense distress.

> ELINOR
> Colonel Brandon, what a pleasure to see you! Have you been in London all this while?

> COLONEL BRANDON
> I have. How is your dear mother?

> ELINOR
> Very well, thank you.

Silence.

> ELINOR
> Colonel, is there anything –

But BRANDON interrupts her.

––––––––

COLONEL BRANDON
Forgive me, Miss Dashwood, but I have heard reports through town . . . is it impossible to – but I could have no chance of succeeding – indeed I hardly know what to do. Tell me once and for all, is everything finally resolved between your sister and Mr Willoughby?

ELINOR *is torn between discomfiture and compassion.*

ELINOR
Colonel, though neither one has informed me of their understanding, I have no doubt of their mutual affection.

BRANDON *stands very still.*

COLONEL BRANDON
Thank you, Miss Dashwood. To your sister I wish all imaginable happiness. To Mr Willoughby, that he . . . may endeavour to deserve her.

His tone is heavy with some bitter meaning.

ELINOR
What do you mean?

But he recollects himself.

COLONEL BRANDON
Forgive me, I – forgive me.

He bows and leaves abruptly. ELINOR *is deeply troubled.*

101 EXT. GREENWICH ARCADE. LONDON. DAY.
The PALMERS, MRS JENNINGS, JOHN, FANNY, LUCY, ELINOR *and* MARIANNE *are walking through the arcade. Additional wealth has evidently encouraged* FANNY *sartorially and she sprouts as much fruit and feathers as a market stall.* LUCY *is holding* ELINOR's *arm in a pinionlike grip.* MRS JENNINGS *is gossiping with* CHARLOTTE. MAR-

---

IANNE's *good looks are heightened by her feverish expectation of seeing* WILLOUGHBY *at every step, and many young men raise their hats to her and turn as she passes.*

MARIANNE
Where is dear Edward, John? We expect to see him daily.

FANNY *stiffens.* LUCY's *sharp eyes dart hither and thither.* MRS JENNINGS *senses gossip.* ELINOR *steels herself.*

MRS JENNINGS
And who is 'dear Edward'?

CHARLOTTE
Who indeed?

FANNY *smiles glacially.*

FANNY
My brother, Mrs Jennings – Edward Ferrars.

MRS JENNINGS *looks at* ELINOR *in sly triumph.*

MRS JENNINGS
Indeed! Is that Ferrars with an F?

She and CHARLOTTE *chuckle to each other.* LUCY *looks at* ELINOR.

102 INT. MRS JENNINGS'S HOUSE. HALL. EVE.
MRS JENNINGS, LUCY, ELINOR *and* MARIANNE *return from their outing.* MARIANNE *immediately assails* PIGEON.

MARIANNE
Are there any messages, Pigeon?

PIGEON
No, ma'am.

MARIANNE
No message at all? No cards?

> PIGEON (*affronted*)
> None, ma'am.

MARIANNE *sighs with disappointment and starts up the stairs. MRS JENNINGS looks archly at ELINOR.*

> MRS JENNINGS
> I note you do not enquire for *your* messages, Miss Dashwood!

> ELINOR
> No, for I do not expect any, Mrs Jennings. I have very little acquaintance in town.

And she follows MARIANNE *firmly upstairs.* LUCY *watches her go, and* MRS JENNINGS *chuckles and turns to her.*

> MRS JENNINGS
> She is as sly as you, Lucy!

103 INT. MRS JENNINGS'S HOUSE. BEDROOM. NIGHT.
ELINOR *wakes up. The flickering of a candle has disturbed her. She sits up in bed and sees* MARIANNE *sitting at the desk in her nightgown, writing another letter.*

> ELINOR
> Marianne, is anything wrong?

> MARIANNE
> Nothing at all. Go back to sleep.

104 INT. MRS JENNINGS'S HOUSE. MORNING ROOM. NIGHT.
MARIANNE, *in her nightclothes and dressing gown, paces restlessly, her letter in her hands. A slight knock at the door heralds a much-ruffled* PIGEON, *wig askew.* MARIANNE *hands him the letter. He bows and goes, highly disgruntled.*

105 INT. MRS JENNINGS'S HOUSE. HALL. MORNING.

MRS JENNINGS *is giving* PIGEON *his instructions for the day.* MAR-
IANNE *comes running downstairs.* PIGEON *regards her drily.*

                          PIGEON
          No messages, ma'am.

MARIANNE *looks so dejected that* MRS JENNINGS *takes her hand.*

                       MRS JENNINGS
          Do not fret, my dear. I am told that this good weather is keeping
          many sportsmen in the country at present, but the frost will
          drive them back to town very soon, depend upon it.

MARIANNE *brightens.*

                          MARIANNE
          Of course! I had not thought of – thank you, Mrs Jennings!

She runs back upstairs. MRS JENNINGS *calls after her.*

                       MRS JENNINGS
          And Miss Dashwood may set her heart at rest, for I overheard
          your sister-in-law say that she was to bring the elusive Mr F to
          the ball tonight!

106 EXT. GRAND CRESCENT LEADING TO BALLROOM
ENTRANCE. NIGHT.
So many carriages have entered the crescent to deliver the GUESTS *that
gridlock has occurred and people are forced to walk to the entrance. We see*
MRS JENNINGS, MARIANNE, ELINOR *and* LUCY *alighting from their
carriage and picking their way through the mud, their skirts raised above
their ankles.* ELINOR *nearly trips and is obliged to grab onto* LUCY *in order
not to slip into the dirt.*

107 INT. GRAND BALLROOM. EVE.
The great ballroom is crammed with GUESTS *all determined to enjoy
themselves despite the considerable inconveniences caused by noise, heat*

and overcrowding. MEN *are sweating profusely,* WOMEN *dab their brows, rack punch is being swallowed by the gallon, flirting is conducted at fever pitch and all conversation is inordinately loud. Only the* DANCERS *have a modicum of space in which to perform their mincing steps.* MRS JENNINGS *and her brood bump into the* PALMERS.

CHARLOTTE (*screeching*)
This is very merry!

MRS JENNINGS *then spots* FANNY, *who is conducting a desultory conversation with an overpowdered* ACQUAINTANCE. *She drags* ELINOR, MARIANNE *and* LUCY *over to her.*

MRS JENNINGS
There you are! Goodness, how hot it is, Mrs Dashwood. You are not alone, I trust?

FANNY
Indeed not. John is just gone to fetch my brother – he has been eating ices.

LUCY *clutches at* ELINOR's *sleeve.*

MRS JENNINGS
Your brother! I declare, that is good news indeed. At long last!

And she beams her approval upon ELINOR.

LUCY (*whispering*)
Miss Dashwood, I declare I shall faint clean away.

FANNY *has seen* JOHN *threading his way towards them and waves at him. There is someone behind him.* LUCY *preens.* JOHN *bows to them.*

JOHN
Mrs Jennings, may I present my brother-in-law?

He turns to reveal a good-looking young MAN *with a vacuous smile.*

JOHN

Mr Robert Ferrars!

ROBERT

My dear ladies – we meet at last!

There is a general bowing and shaking of hands. ELINOR *is relieved.* LUCY *drops a low curtsy.*

MRS JENNINGS

So you must be the younger brother? Is Mr Edward not here? Miss Dashwood here was counting on him!

ROBERT *looks* ELINOR *up and down. He exchanges glances with* FANNY *before he speaks.*

ROBERT

Oh! He is far too busy for such gatherings – and has no special acquaintance here to make his attendance worthwhile.

MRS JENNINGS *looks at* ELINOR *in puzzlement.*

MRS JENNINGS

Well, I declare, I do not know what the young men are about these days – are they all in hiding?

ELINOR *looks down, agonised with embarrassment.*

MRS JENNINGS

Come, Mr Robert, in the absence of your brother, *you* must dance with our lovely Miss Dashwood!

ROBERT (*not best pleased*)

It would be my honour.

He turns to LUCY *and bows.*

ROBERT

And perhaps Miss Steele might consider reserving the allemande?

———

LUCY *curtsies again.* ROBERT *escorts a most unwilling* ELINOR *onto the dance floor.*

ROBERT
You reside in Devonshire, I b'lieve, Miss Dashwood?

ELINOR
We do.

ROBERT
In a cottage?

ELINOR
Yes.

ROBERT
I am excessively fond of a cottage. If I had any money to spare, I should build one myself.

Luckily for ELINOR *the set changes and she is obliged to turn away from* ROBERT. *She wheels round to face her new partner. It is* WILLOUGHBY! *They both stop dancing and stare at each other aghast. A traffic jam starts and they are forced to take hands and resume the steps.*

WILLOUGHBY (*stiff*)
How do you do, Miss Dashwood?

ELINOR *does not know quite how to respond.*

ELINOR
I am well, thank you, Mr Willoughby.

She looks about for MARIANNE, *instinctively wanting to keep her away from* WILLOUGHBY.

WILLOUGHBY
How is your – family?

————

ELINOR (*cold*)
We are all extremely well, Mr Willoughby – thank you for your kind enquiry.

WILLOUGHBY *is shamed into silence. Then he sees* MARIANNE. *At the same moment the music pauses.* MARIANNE *looks up. In the brief moment of relative quiet, her great cry rings across the room.*

MARIANNE
Willoughby!

Everyone turns to look as MARIANNE *rushes towards him with both arms outstretched, her face luminous with joy. As the noise of the room builds again and* PEOPLE *change their partners, we are aware that many are surreptitiously watching.* MARIANNE *reaches him but* WILLOUGHBY *stands with his arms frozen at his side.* MARIANNE *gives a little confused laugh.*

MARIANNE
Good God, Willoughby! Will you not shake hands with me?

WILLOUGHBY *looks extremely uncomfortable and glances towards a group of very smart* PEOPLE *who are watching him closely. Central to this group is a* SOPHISTICATED WOMAN *who frowns at him proprietorially.*

WILLOUGHBY *shakes* MARIANNE's *hand briefly. Behind her,* MRS JENNINGS *is giving an animated commentary to* FANNY *and* JOHN, *while* LUCY *whispers in* ROBERT's *ear as they go past to join the set.*

WILLOUGHBY (*strangled*)
How do you do, Miss Marianne?

MARIANNE
Willoughby, what is the matter? Why have you not come to see me? Were you not in London? Have you not received my letters?

WILLOUGHBY *is sweating with tension.*

> WILLOUGHBY
>
> Yes, I had the pleasure of receiving the information which you were so good as to send me.

> MARIANNE (*piteously*)
>
> For heaven's sake, Willoughby, tell me what is wrong!

> WILLOUGHBY
>
> Thank you – I am most obliged. If you will excuse me, I must return to my party.

He bows, white to the teeth, and walks away to join the SOPHISTICATED WOMAN.

> MARIANNE
>
> Willoughby!

He is drawn away by his PARTY, *some of whom look back at* MARIANNE *with a mixture of curiosity and condescension.* MARIANNE *almost sinks to her knees.* ELINOR *supports her.*

ELINOR

Marianne! Come away!

MARIANNE

Go to him, Elinor – force him to come to me.

MRS JENNINGS *has come up, full of concern.*

ELINOR

Dearest, do not betray what you feel to everyone present! This is not the place for explanations –

MRS JENNINGS

Come along, dear.

They almost have to drag MARIANNE *away.* MRS JENNINGS *turns back to the* DASHWOOD *party.* FANNY *and* JOHN *have practically imploded with embarrassment and are distancing themselves as much as possible from the source.* LUCY *and* ROBERT *are dancing nearby.*

MRS JENNINGS

Will you come, Lucy?

LUCY

Oh, are we leaving so soon?

ROBERT

If I might be so bold, Mrs Jennings, it would be our pleasure to escort your young charge home.

LUCY

How very kind!

MRS JENNINGS

That is very handsome –

———

She rushes off to follow MARIANNE *and* ELINOR. *We stay for a moment with* LUCY *and* ROBERT *who have left the set.*

                    ROBERT
        She actually sent him messages during the night?

CAM rises to show the DASHWOODS *exiting past the whispering, sneering faces of the* CROWD.

108 INT. MRS JENNINGS'S HOUSE. BEDROOM. NIGHT.
MARIANNE *sits scribbling a letter at the desk.*

                    ELINOR
        Marianne, please tell me –

                    MARIANNE
        Do not ask me questions!

                    ELINOR
        You have no confidence in me.

                    MARIANNE
        This reproach from you! You, who confide in no one.

                    ELINOR
        I have nothing to tell.

                    MARIANNE
        Nor I. We have neither of us anything to tell. I because I conceal
        nothing and you because you communicate nothing.

109 INT. MRS JENNINGS'S HOUSE. BREAKFAST ROOM. DAY.
A silent breakfast. MARIANNE *is red-eyed from crying and limp from lack of sleep.* MRS JENNINGS *is dressed to go out, pulling on her gloves and bustling as usual.* PIGEON *enters with a letter on a salver. He offers it to* MARIANNE. *She seizes it and runs out of the room.* MRS JENNINGS *chuckles.*

———

MRS JENNINGS

There now! Lovers' quarrels are swift to heal! That letter will do the trick, mark my word.

She goes to the door.

MRS JENNINGS

I must be off. I hope he won't keep her waiting much longer, Miss Dashwood. It hurts to see her looking so forlorn.

She leaves and ELINOR *finds herself alone with* LUCY, *who loses no time in sharing her new-found happiness.*

LUCY

What a welcome I had from Edward's family, Miss Dashwood – I am surprised you never told me what an agreeable woman your sister-in-law is! And Mr Robert – all so affable!

ELINOR

It is perhaps fortunate that none of them knows of your engagement. Excuse me.

ELINOR *rises and leaves.*

110 INT. MRS JENNINGS'S HOUSE. BEDROOM. DAY.
ELINOR *finds* MARIANNE *sitting on the edge of the bed. She does not acknowledge* ELINOR *but merely lifts the letter and reads out, with deadly calm:*

MARIANNE

'My dear Madam – I am quite at a loss to discover in what point I could be so unfortunate as to offend you. My esteem for your family is very sincere but if I have given rise to a belief of more than I felt or meant to express, I shall reproach myself for not having been more guarded. My affections have long been engaged elsewhere and it is with great regret that I return your letters and the lock of hair

---

147

which you so obligingly bestowed upon me. I am etc. John Willoughby.'

ELINOR

Oh, Marianne.

MARIANNE *gives a great howl of pain and flings herself across the bed as though in physical agony.*

ELINOR

Marianne, oh, Marianne – it is better to know at once what his intentions are. Dearest, think of what you would have felt if your engagement had carried on for months and months before he chose to put an end to it.

MARIANNE

We are not engaged.

ELINOR

But you wrote to him! I thought then that he must have left you with some kind of understanding?

MARIANNE

No – he is not so unworthy as you think him.

ELINOR

Not so unworthy! Did he tell you that he loved you?

MARIANNE

Yes. No – never absolutely. It was every day implied, but never declared. Sometimes I thought it had been, but it never was. He has broken no vow.

ELINOR

He has broken faith with all of us, he made us all believe he loved you.

MARIANNE
He did! He did – he loved me as I loved him.

MRS JENNINGS *bursts through the door in her hat and coat, panting.*

MRS JENNINGS
I had to come straight up – how are you, Miss Marianne?

MARIANNE *begins to sob uncontrollably.*

MRS JENNINGS
Poor thing! She looks very bad. No wonder, Miss Dashwood, for it is but too true. I was told here in the street by Miss Morton, who is a great friend: he is to be married at the end of the month – to a Miss Grey with fifty thousand pounds. Well, said I, if 'tis true, then he is a good-for-nothing who has used my young friend abominably ill, and I wish with all my soul that his wife may plague his heart out!

She goes round the bed to comfort MARIANNE.

MRS JENNINGS
But he is not the only young man worth having, my dear, and with your pretty face you will never want for admirers.

MARIANNE *sobs even harder.*

MRS JENNINGS
Ah, me! She had better have her cry out and have done with it. I will go and look out something to tempt her – does she care for olives?

ELINOR
I cannot tell you.

MRS JENNINGS *leaves.* MARIANNE *seizes the letter again.*

MARIANNE
I cannot believe his nature capable of such cruelty!

———

ELINOR

Marianne, there is no excuse for him – this is his hand –

MARIANNE

But it cannot be his heart! Oh, Mamma! I want Mamma! Elinor, please take me home! Cannot we go tomorrow?

ELINOR

There is no one to take us.

MARIANNE

Cannot we hire a carriage?

ELINOR

We have no money – and indeed we owe Mrs Jennings more courtesy.

MARIANNE

All *she* wants is gossip and she only likes me because I supply it! Oh, God! I cannot endure to stay.

ELINOR

I will find a way. I promise.

111 INT. COFFEE-HOUSE. COVENT GARDEN. DAY.
FANNY, JOHN *and* ROBERT *are drinking chocolate together.*

ROBERT

Apparently they never were engaged.

FANNY

Miss Grey has fifty thousand pounds. Marianne is virtually penniless.

JOHN

She cannot have expected him to go through with it. But I feel for Marianne – she will lose her bloom and end a spinster like Elinor. I think, my dear, we might consider having them to stay

---

150

with us for a few days – we are, after all, family, and my father . . .

He trails off. FANNY *exchanges an alarmed glance with* ROBERT. *She thinks fast.*

FANNY
My love, I would ask them with all my heart, but I have already asked Miss Steele for a visit and we cannot deprive Mrs Jennings of all her company at once. We can invite your sisters some other year, you know, and Miss Steele will profit far more from your generosity – poor girl!

JOHN
That is very thoughtful, Fanny. We shall ask Elinor and Marianne next year, then . . .

FANNY

Certainly!

112 EXT. JOHN AND FANNY'S TOWN HOUSE. LONDON STREET.
DAY.
MRS JENNINGS's *carriage stands outside. A liveried* FOOTMAN *opens the door and* LUCY *steps out brandishing a new muff.*

115B INT. MRS JENNINGS'S HOUSE. BEDROOM. DAY.
MARIANNE *sits alone on the bed. Around her lie her notes to Willoughby, her lock of hair and the pocket sonnets. In her hands is the creased and tear-stained letter from Willoughby which she is examining over and over.*

114 INT. MRS JENNINGS'S HOUSE. DRAWING ROOM. DAY.
ELINOR *is seated at a desk writing a letter. There is a sudden rap at the front door. Footsteps are heard and as she turns, the maid enters with* COLONEL BRANDON. ELINOR *rises to greet him.*

ELINOR
Thank you for coming, Colonel.

He bows. ELINOR *is on edge.* BRANDON *looks haggard with concern.*

COLONEL BRANDON
How does your sister?

ELINOR
I must get her home as quickly as possible. The Palmers can take us as far as Cleveland, which is but a day from Barton –

COLONEL BRANDON
Then permit me to accompany you and take you straight on from Cleveland to Barton myself.

ELINOR *takes his hands gratefully.*

ELINOR
I confess that is precisely what I had hoped for. Marianne

---

suffers cruelly, and what pains me most is how hard she tries to justify Mr Willoughby. But you know her disposition.

After a moment BRANDON *nods. He seems unable to remain still or calm and finds it difficult to begin speaking.*

COLONEL BRANDON

Perhaps I – my regard for you all – Miss Dashwood, will you allow me to prove it by relating some circumstances which nothing but an earnest desire of being useful –

ELINOR

You have something to tell me of Mr Willoughby.

COLONEL BRANDON (*nods*)

When I quitted Barton last – but I must go further back. A short account of myself will be necessary. No doubt . . . no doubt Mrs Jennings has apprised you of certain events in my past – the sad outcome of my connection with a young woman named Eliza.

ELINOR *nods.*

COLONEL BRANDON

What is *not* commonly known is that twenty years ago, Eliza bore an illegitimate child. The father, whoever he was, abandoned them.

This is strong stuff. ELINOR's *concern deepens.*

COLONEL BRANDON

As she lay dying, she begged me to look after the child. Eliza died in my arms, broken, wasted away – ah! Miss Dashwood, such a subject – untouched for so many years – it is dangerous . . .

He paces about, barely able to conceal his distress.

COLONEL BRANDON

I had failed Eliza in every other way – I could not refuse her

---

153

now. I took the child – Beth is her name – and placed her with a family where I could be sure she would be well looked after. I saw her whenever I could. I saw that she was headstrong like her mother – and, God forgive me, I indulged her, I allowed her too much freedom. Almost a year ago, she disappeared.

ELINOR

Disappeared!

COLONEL BRANDON

I instigated a search but for eight months I was left to imagine the worst. At last, on the day of the Delaford picnic, I received the first news her. She was with child . . . and the blackguard who had –

BRANDON *stops and looks straight at* ELINOR.

ELINOR

Good God. Do you mean – Willoughby?

BRANDON *nods.* ELINOR *drops into a chair, utterly shocked.*

COLONEL BRANDON

Before I could return to confront him, Lady Allen learned of his behaviour and turned him from the house. He beat a hasty retreat to London –

ELINOR

Yes! He left us that morning, without any explanation!

COLONEL BRANDON

Lady Allen had annulled his legacy. He was left with next to nothing, and in danger of losing all that remained to his debtors –

ELINOR

– and so abandoned Marianne for Miss Grey and her fifty thousand pounds.

BRANDON *is silent.* ELINOR *is breathless.*

ELINOR

Have you seen Mr Willoughby since you learned . . .?

BRANDON (*nodding*)

We met by appointment, he to defend, I to punish his conduct.

ELINOR *stares at him, aghast.*

BRANDON

We returned unwounded, so the meeting never got abroad.

ELINOR *nods and is silent for a moment.*

ELINOR

Is Beth still in town?

COLONEL BRANDON

She has chosen to go into the country for her confinement. Such has been the unhappy resemblance between the fate of mother and daughter, and so imperfectly have I discharged my trust.

A pause.

COLONEL BRANDON

I would not have burdened you, Miss Dashwood, had I not from my heart believed it might, in time, lessen your sister's regrets.

BRANDON *moves to the door and then stops. He turns to her and speaks with effort.*

COLONEL BRANDON

I have described Mr Willoughby as the worst of libertines – but I have since learned from Lady Allen that he did mean to propose that day. Therefore I cannot deny that his intentions towards Marianne *were* honourable, and I feel certain he would have married her, had it not been for –

———

ELINOR

For the money.

She looks up at BRANDON. Silence.

115 INT. MRS JENNINGS'S HOUSE. BEDROOM. NIGHT.
MARIANNE *is sitting on the bed staring into space.* ELINOR *is kneeling by
her, holding her hands.*

ELINOR

Dearest, was I right to tell you?

MARIANNE

Of course.

ELINOR

Whatever his past actions, whatever his present course, at least
you may be certain that he loved you.

MARIANNE

But not enough. Not enough.

115A INT. MRS JENNINGS'S HOUSE. STUDY. DAY.
ELINOR *sits alone with her head in her hands. Suddenly* MRS JENNINGS
bustles in looking pleased.

MRS JENNINGS

Here is someone to cheer you up, Miss Dashwood!

She is followed in by LUCY. MRS JENNINGS *leaves, busy as ever.* LUCY
plants an expression of ghastly concern on her face.

LUCY

How is your dear sister, Miss Dashwood? Poor thing! I must
say, I do not know what I should do if a man treated me with so
little respect.

ELINOR

I hope you are enjoying your stay with John and Fanny, Miss Steele?

LUCY

I was never so happy in my entire life, Miss Dashwood! I do believe your sister-in-law has taken quite a fancy to me. I had to come and tell you – for you cannot *imagine* what has happened!

ELINOR

No, I cannot.

LUCY

Yesterday I was introduced to Edward's mother!

ELINOR

Indeed?

LUCY

And she was a vast deal more than civil. I have not yet seen Edward but now I feel sure to very soon –

The MAID *comes back.*

MAID
There's a Mr Edward Ferrars to see you, Miss Dashwood.

There is a tiny frozen silence.

ELINOR
Do ask him to come up.

ELINOR *quite involuntarily sits down and then stands up again.* EDWARD
is admitted, looking both anxious and eager. As LUCY *is sitting in the
window seat, at first he sees only* ELINOR.

EDWARD
Miss Dashwood, how can I –

But ELINOR *cuts him off.*

ELINOR
Mr Ferrars, what a pleasure to see you. You . . . know Miss
Steele, of course.

EDWARD *turns slowly and encounters* LUCY's *glassy smile. He all but
blenches. Then bows, and clears his throat.*

EDWARD
How do you do, Miss Steele.

LUCY
I am well, thank you, Mr Ferrars.

EDWARD *has no notion of what to do or say. He swallows.*

ELINOR
Do sit down, Mr Ferrars.

LUCY's *eyes are sharp as broken glass.* EDWARD *remains on his feet,
looking helplessly from one woman to the other.*

LUCY

You must be surprised to find me here, Mr Ferrars! I expect you thought I was at your sister's house.

This is precisely what EDWARD *had thought. He tries to smile but his facial muscles won't work.* ELINOR *decides to fetch help.*

ELINOR

Let me call Marianne, Mr Ferrars. She would be most disappointed to miss you.

ELINOR *goes to the door, thankful to escape, but* MARIANNE *prevents her by walking in at that moment. Despite her anguish, she is very pleased to see* EDWARD *and embraces him warmly.*

MARIANNE

Edward! I heard your voice! At last you have found us!

EDWARD *is shocked by her appearance and momentarily forgets his own confusion.*

EDWARD

Forgive me, Marianne, my visit is shamefully overdue. You are pale. I hope you have not been unwell?

MARIANNE

Oh, don't think of me – Elinor is well, you see, that must be enough for both of us!

MARIANNE *gestures to* ELINOR *encouragingly but* EDWARD *seems unable to look at her.*

EDWARD

How do you like London, Marianne?

MARIANNE

Not at all. The sight of you is all the pleasure it has afforded, is that not so, Elinor?

Again, MARIANNE *endeavours to ignite the lovers.* ELINOR *tries to silence* MARIANNE *with her eyes but to no avail.* MARIANNE *puts their coolness down to the presence of* LUCY, *at whom she glances with a none too friendly air.*

MARIANNE

Why have you taken so long to come and see us?

EDWARD

I have been much engaged elsewhere.

MARIANNE

Engaged elsewhere! But what was that when there were such friends to be met?

LUCY

Perhaps, Miss Marianne, you think young men never honour their engagements, little or great.

21

23

27

28

31

35

ELINOR *is appalled by this remark but* MARIANNE *does not notice it and turns back to* LUCY *earnestly.*

MARIANNE

No, indeed – for Edward is the most fearful of giving pain and the most incapable of being selfish of anyone I ever saw.

EDWARD *makes an uncomfortable noise.*

MARIANNE

Edward, will you not sit? Elinor, help me to persuade him.

Now EDWARD *can stand it no longer.*

EDWARD

Forgive me but I must take my leave –

MARIANNE

But you are only just arrived!

ELINOR *rises, desperate for them both to go.*

EDWARD

You must excuse me, I have a commission to attend to for Fanny –

LUCY *jumps in like a shot.*

LUCY

In that case perhaps you might escort me back to your sister's house, Mr Ferrars?

There is an extremely awkward pause.

EDWARD

I would be honoured. Goodbye, Miss Dashwood, Miss Marianne.

He shakes hands with ELINOR *and with* MARIANNE, *who is silent with dismay.* LUCY *takes* EDWARD's *arm and looks up at him proprietorially.*

———

After a stiff bow and a muttered farewell from EDWARD, *they leave.*
MARIANNE *looks at her sister in astonishment.*

> MARIANNE
> Why did you not urge him to stay?

> ELINOR
> He must have had his reasons for going.

> MARIANNE
> His reason was no doubt your coldness. If I were Edward I
> would assume you did not care for me at all.

117 EXT. JOHN AND FANNY'S TOWN HOUSE. BACK GARDEN.
DAY.
A tranquil afternoon . . .

118 INT. JOHN AND FANNY'S TOWN HOUSE. DRAWING ROOM.
DAY.
LUCY *is sitting with* FANNY, *who is doing some pointless basketwork.*
LUCY *hands* FANNY *rushes.*

> LUCY
> Poor Miss Marianne looked very badly t'other day. When I
> think of her, deserted and abandoned, it frightens me to think I
> shall never marry.

> FANNY
> Nonsense. You will marry far better than either of the Dash-
> wood girls.

> LUCY
> How can that possibly be?

> FANNY
> You have ten times their sense and looks.

                    LUCY

But I have no dowry.

                    FANNY

There are qualities which will always make up for that, and you
have them in abundance. It would not surprise me if you were
to marry far and away beyond your expectations.

                    LUCY

I wish it might be so. There is a young man –

                    FANNY

Ah ha! I am glad to hear of it. Is he of good breeding and
fortune?

                    LUCY

Oh both – but his family would certainly oppose the match.

                    FANNY

Tush! They will allow it as soon as they see you, my dear.

                    LUCY

It is a very great secret. I have told no one in the world for fear
of discovery.

FANNY *looks up, curious to know more.*

                    FANNY

My dear, I am the soul of discretion.

                    LUCY

If I dared tell . . .

                    FANNY

I can assure you I am as silent as the grave.

LUCY *leans forward to whisper in* FANNY's *ear.*

119 EXT. JOHN AND FANNY'S TOWN HOUSE. DAY.

—————

We hold a long shot of the house for a moment of silence. Then from inside comes an almost inhumanly loud shriek.

FANNY (V/O)

Viper in my bosom!

120 EXT. JOHN AND FANNY'S TOWN HOUSE. BACK GARDEN. DAY.

FANNY *is trying to drag* LUCY *out of the house.* ROBERT *and* JOHN *are trying to reason with her.* FANNY *loses her grip and falls backwards.* LUCY *flings herself into* ROBERT'*s arms.* ROBERT *falls over.*

121 EXT. LONDON STREET. DAY.

MRS JENNINGS *is running as fast as her fat little legs will carry her.*

122 EXT. MRS JENNINGS'S HOUSE. BERKELEY STREET. DAY.

MRS JENNINGS *pants up the front steps.*

123 INT. MRS JENNINGS'S HOUSE. BEDROOM. DAY.

ELINOR *and* MARIANNE *are packing. Their mood is gloomy and uncommunicative.* MRS JENNINGS *explodes into the room fighting for breath.*

> MRS JENNINGS
> Oh, my dears! What a commotion! Mr Edward Ferrars – the very one I used to joke *you* about, Miss Dashwood – has been engaged these five years to Lucy Steele!

MARIANNE *lets out a gasp. She looks at* ELINOR, *who nods at her in swift confirmation.*

> MRS JENNINGS
> Poor Mr Ferrars! His mother, who by all accounts is very proud, demanded that he break the engagement on pain of disinheritance. But he has refused to break his promise to Lucy. He has stood by her, good man, and is cut off without a penny! She has settled it all irrevocably upon Mr Robert. But I cannot stop, I must go to Lucy. Your sister-in-law scolded her like any fury – drove her to hysterics . . .

She leaves the room, still rabbiting on. There is a silence.

> MARIANNE
> How long have you known?

> ELINOR
> Since the evening Mrs Jennings offered to take us to London.

> MARIANNE
> Why did you not tell me?

> ELINOR
> Lucy told me in the strictest confidence.

MARIANNE *looks at her in complete incredulity.*

ELINOR

I could *not* break my word.

Clearly, there is no arguing this point.

MARIANNE

But Edward loves *you.*

ELINOR

He made me no promises. He tried to tell me about Lucy.

MARIANNE

He cannot marry her.

ELINOR

Would you have him treat her even worse than Willoughby has
treated you?

MARIANNE
No – but nor would I have him marry where he does not love.

ELINOR *tries hard to be controlled.*

ELINOR
Edward made his promise a long time ago, long before he met me. Though he may . . . harbour some regret, I believe he will be happy – in the knowledge that he did his duty and kept his word. After all – after all that is bewitching in the idea of one's happiness depending entirely on one person, it is not always possible. We must accept. Edward will marry Lucy – and you and I will go home.

MARIANNE
Always resignation and acceptance! Always prudence and honour and duty! Elinor, where is your heart?

ELINOR *finally explodes. She turns upon* MARIANNE *almost savagely.*

ELINOR
What do you know of my heart? What do you know of anything but your own suffering? For weeks, Marianne, I have had this pressing on me without being at liberty to speak of it to a single creature. It was forced upon me by the very person whose prior claims ruined all my hopes. I have had to endure her exultation again and again while knowing myself to be divided from Edward forever. Believe me, Marianne, had I not been bound to silence I could have produced proof enough of a broken heart even for you.

Complete silence. Then MARIANNE *speaks in a whisper.*

MARIANNE
Oh, Elinor!

MARIANNE *bursts into sobs and flings her arms around* ELINOR, *who, almost impatiently, tries to comfort her.*

---

124 EXT. PALMER RESIDENCE. LONDON STREET. DAY.
LUCY *and* MRS JENNINGS *are on the doorstep.* LUCY *looks rather lost and pathetic, with her little bundles, hastily packed. The door opens and* CHARLOTTE *precedes the* SERVANT, *ushering them in with shrill cries of sympathy.*

> COLONEL BRANDON (V/O)
> I have heard that your friend Mr Ferrars has been entirely cast off by his family for persevering in his engagement to Miss Steele . . .

125 EXT. SQUARE IN FRONT OF MRS JENNINGS'S HOUSE. LONDON. DAY.
ELINOR *and* BRANDON *walk round the quiet square.*

> COLONEL BRANDON (*cont.*)
> Have I been rightly informed? Is it so?

ELINOR *is greatly taken aback by this unexpected query.*

> ELINOR
> It is indeed so. Are you acquainted with Mr Ferrars?

> COLONEL BRANDON
> No, we have never met. But I know only too well the cruelty – the *impolitic* cruelty of dividing two young people long attached to one another. Mrs Ferrars does not know what she may drive her son to –

He pauses, frowning in remembrance. ELINOR *waits in suspense.*

> COLONEL BRANDON
> I have a proposal to make that should enable him to marry Miss Steele immediately. Since the gentleman is so close a friend to your family, perhaps you will be good enough to mention it to him?

ELINOR *is completely taken aback. She takes a moment to reply.*

> ELINOR
>
> Colonel, I am sure he would be only too delighted to hear it from your own lips.

> COLONEL BRANDON
>
> I think not. His behaviour has proved him proud – in the best sense. I feel certain this is the right course.

126 INT. MRS JENNINGS'S HOUSE. STUDY. DAY.

ELINOR *is waiting. The* MAID *announces* EDWARD *and he walks in momentarily. They are alone for the first time in months and for a moment, neither speaks.*

> ELINOR
>
> Mr Ferrars.

> EDWARD
>
> Miss Dashwood.

ELINOR *indicates a seat for him but neither sits.*

> ELINOR
>
> Thank you for responding so promptly to my message.

> EDWARD
>
> I was most grateful to receive it. I – Miss Dashwood, God knows what you must think of me . . .

> ELINOR
>
> Mr Ferrars –

He interrupts her, desperate to explain.

> EDWARD
>
> I have no right to speak, I know –

ELINOR *has to stop him.*

ELINOR

Mr Ferrars, I have good news. I think you know of our friend
Colonel Brandon?

EDWARD *looks completely bewildered.*

EDWARD

Yes, I have heard his name.

ELINOR *starts to speak rather faster than usual.*

ELINOR

Colonel Brandon desires me to say that, understanding you
wish to join the clergy, he has great pleasure in offering you the
parish on his estate at Delaford, now just vacant, in the hope
that it may enable you – and Miss Steele – to marry.

EDWARD *cannot at first take it in.* ELINOR *sits down.*

EDWARD

Colonel Brandon?

ELINOR

Yes. He means it as testimony of his concern for – for the cruel
situation in which you find yourselves.

Now EDWARD *sits – in shock.*

EDWARD

Colonel Brandon give *me* a parish? Can it be possible?

ELINOR

The unkindness of your family has made you astonished to find
friendship elsewhere.

EDWARD *looks at* ELINOR, *his eyes full of growing comprehension.*

EDWARD

No. Not to find it in you. I cannot be ignorant that to you – to

---

your goodness – I owe it all. I feel it. I would express it if I could, but, as you know, I am no orator.

ELINOR

You are very much mistaken. I assure you that you owe it almost entirely to your own merit – I have had no hand in it.

But EDWARD *clearly believes she has been instrumental in the offer. He frowns slightly before speaking with rather an effort.*

EDWARD

Colonel Brandon must be a man of great worth and respectability.

ELINOR *finds some relief in saying at least one thing that she truly means.*

ELINOR

He is the kindest and best of men.

This makes EDWARD *seem even more depressed. He sits silent for a moment but then rouses himself to action.*

EDWARD

May I enquire why the Colonel did not tell me himself?

ELINOR

I think he felt it would be better coming from . . . a friend.

EDWARD *looks at* ELINOR, *his eyes full of sadness.*

EDWARD

Your friendship has been the most important of my life.

ELINOR

You will always have it.

EDWARD

Forgive me.

———

ELINOR

Mr Ferrars, you honour your promises – that is more important than anything else. I wish you – both – very happy.

They rise. She curtsies. He bows.

EDWARD

Goodbye, Miss Dashwood.

EDWARD *leaves silently.* ELINOR *stands stock-still in the middle of the room.*

127 EXT. MRS JENNINGS'S HOUSE. DAY.
The PALMERS' *carriage stands outside the house.* COLONEL BRANDON *helps* MARIANNE *in beside* ELINOR *before mounting his horse to ride alongside.* MRS JENNINGS *waves goodbye from the steps. The carriage moves off.* MRS JENNINGS *blows her nose, looks up and down the street in search of gossip and goes back indoors with a sigh.*

128 INT. THE PALMERS' CARRIAGE. ON THE ROAD. DAY.
MARIANNE *is sitting back in her seat with her eyes closed. She does not look well.* MR PALMER *is behind his newspaper.*

> CHARLOTTE
> What a stroke of luck for Lucy and Edward to find a parish so close to Barton! You will all be able to meet very often. That will cheer you up, Miss Marianne. I do declare I have never disliked a person so much as I do Mr Willoughby, for your sake. Insufferable man! To think we can see his insufferable house from the top of our hill!

CLOSE *on* MARIANNE'*s eyes slowly opening.*

> CHARLOTTE
> I shall ask Jackson to plant some very tall trees.

> MR PALMER (*from behind the paper*)
> You will do nothing of the sort.

129 EXT. THE PALMERS' CARRIAGE. OPEN ROAD. DAY.
The carriage bowls along, with BRANDON *riding next to it.*

> CHARLOTTE (V/O)
> I hear Miss Grey's bridal gown was everything of the finest – made in Paris, no less. I should have liked to see it, although I dare say it was a sorry affair, scalloped with ruffles – but what do the French know about fashion?

130 EXT. CLEVELAND. DRIVE. AFTERNOON.
The carriage stands outside the PALMER *residence, a resplendent affair with a great deal of land.* BRANDON *is helping* MARIANNE *and* ELINOR *out of the carriage.*

> CHARLOTTE (V/O)
> I am resolved never to mention Mr Willoughby's name again, and furthermore I shall tell everyone I meet what a good-for-nothing he is.

MR PALMER (V/O)
Be quiet.

ELINOR *and* MARIANNE *stand on the steps as the* PALMERS *debouch from the carriage amid a welter of* SERVANTS.

ELINOR *(sotto voce)*
I do not think she drew breath from the moment we left London. It is my fault – I should have found some other way of getting home.

MARIANNE
There was no other way – you said so yourself.

ELINOR
We shall be home soon enough. Mamma will comfort you, dearest.

MARIANNE
I am stiff from sitting so long. Will you tell Charlotte that I am going for a stroll?

ELINOR *glances at the sky in concern.*

ELINOR
I think it is going to rain.

MARIANNE
No, no, it will not rain.

ELINOR *cannot help but smile at this return of the old* MARIANNE.

ELINOR
You always say that and then it always does.

MARIANNE
I will keep to the garden, near the house.

MARIANNE *walks off.* ELINOR *watches her go anxiously.*

132 INT. CLEVELAND. DRAWING ROOM. DAY.
MRS BUNTING, *a rather baleful* NANNY, *looks on as* MR PALMER *holds up a screaming* BABY *in a frilly bonnet for everyone's inspection.*

> CHARLOTTE
> We are very proud of our little Thomas, Colonel – and his papa has such a way with him . . .

BRANDON *flicks a glance at* MR PALMER *for whom holding a baby comes as naturally as breathing underwater.*

133 EXT. CLEVELAND. GARDEN. DAY.
MARIANNE *walks purposefully towards the garden wall, beyond which lies a hill.*

134 INT. CLEVELAND. DRAWING ROOM. DAY.
ELINOR *enters to find* CHARLOTTE *alone with the now hysterical* BABY THOMAS.

> CHARLOTTE
> There you are, Miss Dashwood! Mr Palmer and the Colonel have locked themselves up in the billiard room. Come and meet little Thomas. Where is Miss Marianne?

> ELINOR
> She is taking a little air in the garden.

> CHARLOTTE
> Oh, very good. That is the great advantage of the countryside – all the fresh air and . . . and all the fresh air . . .

CHARLOTTE's *conversational difficulties are drowned out by her offspring.*

135 EXT. CLEVELAND. GARDEN. DAY.
MARIANNE *comes to a gate in the wall and turns the handle. It opens. She throws a glance back to the house and passes through. There is a low rumble of thunder.*

---

136 INT. CLEVELAND. DRAWING ROOM. DAY.
BABY THOMAS *is purple in the face but shows no signs of quietening.*
CHARLOTTE *joggles him about inefficiently.*

> CHARLOTTE (*yelling*)
> He is the best child in the world – he never cries unless he wants
> to and then, Lord, there is no stopping him.

137 EXT. THE HILL. DAY.
MARIANNE, *calm and determined, walks towards the top of the hill. The
wind whips and plucks at her hair and skirts.*

138 INT. CLEVELAND. DRAWING ROOM. DAY.
ELINOR, *traumatised by her new acquaintance with the shrieking* BABY
THOMAS, *goes to look out of the window. She frowns.*

139 EXT. CLEVELAND. GARDEN. DAY.
ELINOR's POV. MARIANNE *is nowhere in sight. Storm clouds have
gathered on the hill.*

140 INT. CLEVELAND. DRAWING ROOM. DAY.
ELINOR *turns from the window.* BABY THOMAS *stops crying for two
seconds.*

> ELINOR
> I cannot see Marianne.

There is a crack of thunder. BABY THOMAS *starts again.*

141 EXT. THE HILL. DAY.
Rain has started to pour down. MARIANNE *walks on regardless.*

142 INT. CLEVELAND. DRAWING ROOM. DAY.
CHARLOTTE *shouts over* BABY THOMAS *to* ELINOR.

> CHARLOTTE
> She has probably taken shelter in one of the greenhouses!

———

143 EXT. THE HILL. DAY.
MARIANNE *has reached the top. Soaked to the skin, she stands with the storm raging around her, staring at the spires of Combe Magna, the place that would have been her home. Rain streaks her face and the wind whips her hair about her. Through frozen lips she whispers:*

> MARIANNE
>
> Love is not love
> Which alters when it alteration finds
> Or bends with the remover to remove:
> O, no! it is an ever-fixed mark
> That looks on tempests and is never shaken . . .

144 EXT. CLEVELAND. GREENHOUSES. DAY.
BRANDON *is looking for* MARIANNE. *He enters a greenhouse.*

> COLONEL BRANDON
>
> Marianne!

145 EXT. THE HILL. DAY.
MARIANNE *stares at Combe Magna, a strange smile playing about her lips. Then she calls to* WILLOUGHBY *as though he were near. The effect is eerie, unworldly.*

> MARIANNE
>
> Willoughby . . . Willoughby . . .

146 INT. CLEVELAND. DRAWING ROOM. DAY.
CHARLOTTE, MR PALMER *and* ELINOR *are waiting anxiously.* BABY THOMAS *has been removed.* ELINOR *is staring out of the window.*

> CHARLOTTE
>
> One thing is certain – she will be wet through when she returns.

> MR PALMER
>
> Thank you for pointing that out, my dear. Do not worry, Miss

Dashwood – Brandon will find her. I think we can all guess where she went.

147 EXT. THE HILL. DAY.
BRANDON *runs up the hillside as though the devil were at his heels.*

148 INT. CLEVELAND. DRAWING ROOM. DAY.
CHARLOTTE *is handing* ELINOR *a cup of tea.* ELINOR *turns back to look out of the window. She freezes.*

149 EXT. CLEVELAND. GARDEN. DAY.
ELINOR's POV *of* BRANDON *walking up to the house with* MARIANNE *cradled in his arms. It is like seeing Willoughby's ghost.*

150 INT. CLEVELAND. HALL. DAY.
Everyone rushes out of the drawing room as the COLONEL *enters with* MARIANNE. *He is exhausted and soaked.* MARIANNE *is dumb with cold and fatigue.*

COLONEL BRANDON
She is not hurt – but we must get her warm!

ELINOR *and* MR PALMER *take* MARIANNE *from* BRANDON *and go upstairs, with* CHARLOTTE *in pursuit.*

151 EXT. CLEVELAND. NIGHT. RAIN.
The great house sits in darkness. A sense of foreboding.

152 INT. CLEVELAND. UPSTAIRS CORRIDOR. NIGHT.
ELINOR *is in her nightgown, knocking at a door.* MR PALMER *answers in his nightshirt, astonished to have been summoned out of bed.*

ELINOR
I think Marianne may need a doctor.

153 INT. CLEVELAND. BREAKFAST ROOM. DAY.
MR PALMER *and* CHARLOTTE *are sitting at the breakfast table.* BRANDON *is pacing. The rain has stopped.*

CHARLOTTE

You'll wear yourself out, Colonel! Do not worry! A day or two in bed will soon set her to rights!

MR PALMER

You can rely upon Harris, Colonel. I have never found a better physician.

Enter ELINOR *with* DR HARRIS.

COLONEL BRANDON (*urgent*)

What is your diagnosis?

DR HARRIS

It is an infectious fever that has taken far more serious hold than I would have expected in one so young. I would recommend the hasty removal of your child, Mr Palmer —

CHARLOTTE *runs out of the room screaming.*

CHARLOTTE

Mrs Bunting! Mrs Bunting!

154 EXT. CLEVELAND. FRONT STEPS. DAY.
CHARLOTTE *is getting into their carriage with* MRS BUNTING *and* BABY THOMAS. MR PALMER *is on the steps with* ELINOR. *He takes her hand and looks at her with real sympathy.*

MR PALMER

My dear Miss Dashwood, I am more sorry than I can say. If you would prefer me to stay I am at your service.

ELINOR *is touched to find this warm heart beneath his frosty exterior.*

ELINOR

Mr Palmer, that is very kind. But Colonel Brandon and Dr Harris will look after us. Thank you for everything you have done.

MR PALMER *nods, presses her hand, and walks down the steps to the carriage.*

155 INT. CLEVELAND. DRAWING ROOM. DAY.
BRANDON *sits head in hands. His ghosts have come to haunt him.*

156. INT. CLEVELAND. ELINOR AND MARIANNE'S BEDROOM. DAY.
MARIANNE *is tossing and turning in the bed.* DR HARRIS *is trying to take her pulse. He looks up at* ELINOR, *who is watching anxiously.*

> DR HARRIS
> She is not doing as well as I would like.

157 INT. CLEVELAND. UPSTAIRS CORRIDOR. DAY.
ELINOR *exits the bedroom to find* BRANDON *outside. She jumps.*

> COLONEL BRANDON
> What can I do?

> ELINOR
> Colonel, you have done so much already.

> COLONEL BRANDON
> Give me an occupation, Miss Dashwood, or I shall run mad.

He is dangerously quiet.

> ELINOR
> She would be easier if her mother were here.

> COLONEL BRANDON
> Of course. Barton is but eight hours away. If I make no stop, you may see us early tomorrow morning.

He takes ELINOR's *hand and kisses it.*

> COLONEL BRANDON
> In your hands I know she will be safe.

---

158 EXT. CLEVELAND. DRIVE. EVE.
BRANDON *mounts his horse, turns to look at the house for a moment, and then spurs it violently forward.*

159 INT. CLEVELAND. ELINOR AND MARIANNE'S BEDROOM. EVE.
ELINOR *is by the window, having watched* BRANDON's *departure.* DR HARRIS *is by* MARIANNE's *side. He turns to* ELINOR.

> DR HARRIS
> Double the number of drops and I will return as soon as I can.

160 EXT. CLEVELAND. NIGHT.
The house stands in virtual darkness with only a dim light issuing from one of the upper rooms.

161 EXT. OPEN ROAD. NIGHT.
BRANDON *riding fast, his cape billowing out behind him.*

162 INT. CLEVELAND. ELINOR AND MARIANNE'S BEDROOM. NIGHT.
MARIANNE's *eyes glitter with the fever.* ELINOR *wipes her brow. Suddenly she speaks.*

> MARIANNE
> Who is that?

She is looking at the end of the bed.

> MARIANNE
> Look, look, Elinor.

> ELINOR
> There is no one there, dearest.

> MARIANNE
> It is Papa. Papa has come.

ELINOR *looks fearfully towards the end of the bed.* MARIANNE *tries to smile with her cracked lips.*

MARIANNE

    Dearest Papa!

The dead are coming for the dying.

DISSOLVE.

163 INT. CLEVELAND. ELINOR AND MARIANNE'S BEDROOM.
LATER.
ELINOR, *her eyes red from watching, wipes* MARIANNE*'s temples.* DR
HARRIS *takes her pulse and looks at* ELINOR *anxiously. His silence is
worse than any utterance.*

DISSOLVE.

164 INT. CLEVELAND. ELINOR AND MARIANNE'S BEDROOM.
LATER.
The room is very still. MARIANNE *is pale as wax.* DR HARRIS *puts on his
coat.* ELINOR *looks at him fearfully.*

DR HARRIS

    I must fetch more laudanum. I cannot pretend, Miss Dashwood,
    that your sister's condition is not very serious. You must
    prepare yourself. I will return very shortly.

He leaves the room.

DISSOLVE.

165 INT. CLEVELAND. ELINOR AND MARIANNE'S BEDROOM.
LATER.
MARIANNE *lies in the grip of her fever.* ELINOR *sits watching her. Slowly
she rises and walks to the bed. When she speaks, her tone is very practical.*

ELINOR

    Marianne, Marianne, please try –

*Suddenly, almost unconsciously, she starts to heave with dry sobs, wrenched out
of her, full of anguish and heartbreak and all the more painful for being tearless.*

––––––––

183

ELINOR

Marianne, please try – I cannot – I cannot do without you. Oh, please, I have tried to bear everything else – I will try – but please, dearest, beloved Marianne, do not leave me alone . . .

She falls to her knees by the bed, gulping for breath, taking MARIANNE's *hand and kissing it again and again.*

DISSOLVE.

166 EXT. CLEVELAND. GARDENS. DAWN.
A shimmer of light appears on the rim of the horizon. Somewhere a lark breaks into clear untroubled song.

167 INT. CLEVELAND. ELINOR AND MARIANNE'S BEDROOM. MORNING.
DR HARRIS *sits slumped in a chair.* MARIANNE *lies motionless.* ELINOR

---

rises with difficulty from the bedside and goes to the window. She is white as paper. The lark sings. Then, from behind, comes the faintest of whispers.

                         MARIANNE (V/O)
        Elinor?

ELINOR *turns with a cry.* DR HARRIS *springs from his seat and examines* MARIANNE. *He then turns to* ELINOR *with a smile of relief and nods. At that moment the sound of carriage wheels is heard on the gravel.*

                              ELINOR
        My mother!

168 EXT. CLEVELAND. FRONT STEPS. MORNING.
BRANDON *helps* MRS DASHWOOD, *who is weak with exhaustion and distress, out of the carriage.*

169 INT. CLEVELAND. STAIRCASE. MORNING.
ELINOR *hurls herself down the stairs. She reaches the door just as* BRANDON *and* MRS DASHWOOD *enter and practically swoons into her mother's arms.*

                              ELINOR
        Mamma! She is out of danger!

170 INT. CLEVELAND. ELINOR AND MARIANNE'S BEDROOM. MORNING.
CLOSE *on* MARIANNE'*s face as* MRS DASHWOOD *kisses her.*

                         MRS DASHWOOD
        There, there, my love, my Marianne.

MARIANNE *opens her eyes and smiles at her mother.* MRS DASHWOOD *takes her gently into her arms.* MARIANNE *suddenly looks anxious. She is too weak to move her head. She whispers with urgent effort.*

                           MARIANNE
        Where is Elinor?

                          ————

ELINOR

I am here, dearest, I am here.

MARIANNE *looks at her with deep relief. Behind the* DASHWOODS, BRANDON *stands at the door, unwilling to intrude on this intimacy. He wipes his eyes and turns away.* MARIANNE *sees and whispers to him.*

MARIANNE

Colonel Brandon.

BRANDON *turns back, his eyes full of tears.* MARIANNE *looks at him for a moment. Then, very quietly:*

MARIANNE

Thank you.

171 EXT. BARTON COTTAGE. GARDEN AND SURROUNDINGS. DAY.

The cottage nestles in the first buds of spring. A piece of rope hangs down from the branches of a tree in the garden. It starts to wave about wildly and we see MARGARET *emerging and climbing down. She has built herself a new tree-house.*

COLONEL BRANDON (V/O)

What though the sea with waves continuall
Doe eate the earth, it is no more at all . . .

172 INT. BARTON COTTAGE. PARLOUR. DAY.

MARIANNE *is on the sofa by the window. She is pale, convalescent and calm. Different somehow. She listens intently as* BRANDON *reads her the poem.*

COLONEL BRANDON

Nor is the earth the lesse, or loseth aught.
For whatsoever from one place doth fall,
Is with the tide unto another brought . . .

We move back to find MRS DASHWOOD *and* ELINOR *at the other end of the room, sewing peacefully.*

MRS DASHWOOD

He certainly is not so dashing as Willoughby but he has a far more pleasing countenance. There was always a something, if you remember, in Willoughby's eyes at times which I did not like.

ELINOR *listens patiently as her mother rewrites history. We cut back to* BRANDON *as he finishes reading.*

COLONEL BRANDON

'For there is nothing lost, but may be found, if sought . . .'

He looks up at MARIANNE. *A soul-breathing glance. She smiles as he closes the book.*

MARIANNE
Shall we continue tomorrow?

COLONEL BRANDON
No – for I must away.

MARIANNE
Away? Where?

COLONEL BRANDON (*teasing*)
That I cannot tell you. It is a secret.

He rises to leave.

MARIANNE (*impulsive*)
But you will not stay away long?

CLOSE *on* BRANDON'*s reaction.*

172A EXT. FIELDS NEAR BARTON COTTAGE. DAY.
ELINOR *and* MARIANNE *are out on a walk. They go very slowly,*
MARIANNE *leaning on* ELINOR'*s arm. Their mood is loving, companionable.*

173 EXT. DOWNS NEAR BARTON COTTAGE. DAY.
ELINOR *and* MARIANNE *walk on. Suddenly,* MARIANNE *stops.*

MARIANNE
There.

She indicates a spot on the ground but ELINOR *can see nothing and is momentarily alarmed.* MARIANNE *gazes at the ground and breathes in deeply.*

MARIANNE
There I fell, and there I first saw Willoughby.

ELINOR
Poor Willoughby. He will always regret you.

MARIANNE

But does it follow that, had he chosen me, he would have been content?

ELINOR *looks at* MARIANNE, *surprised.*

MARIANNE

He would have had a wife he loved but no money – and might soon have learned to rank the demands of his pocket-book far above the demands of his heart.

ELINOR *regards* MARIANNE *admiringly.* MARIANNE *smiles sadly.*

MARIANNE

If his present regrets are half as painful as mine, he will suffer enough.

ELINOR

Do you compare your conduct with his?

MARIANNE

No. I compare it with what it ought to have been. I compare it with yours.

ELINOR

Our situations were very different.

MARIANNE

My illness has made me consider the past. I saw in my own behaviour nothing but imprudence – and worse. I was insolent and unjust to everyone –

ELINOR *tries to stem the flow but* MARIANNE *continues.*

MARIANNE

– but you – you I wronged above all. Only I knew your heart and its sorrows but even then I was never a grain more compassionate. I brought my illness upon myself – I wanted

———

189

to destroy myself. And had I succeeded, what misery should I have caused you?

ELINOR *embraces her. They stand with their arms round one another in silence for a moment. Then* MARIANNE *breaks away and speaks with great good humour and energy.*

MARIANNE
I shall mend my ways! I shall no longer worry others nor torture myself. I am determined to enter on a course of serious study – Colonel Brandon has promised me the run of his library and I shall read at least six hours a day. By the end of the year I expect to have improved my learning a very great deal.

174 EXT. ROAD NEAR BARTON COTTAGE. DAY.
THOMAS *is sitting on the back of a local wagon, holding a basket of food. He jumps off near the cottage and waves a cheery farewell to the* DRIVER.

175 INT. BARTON COTTAGE. PARLOUR. DAY.
CLOSE *on the accounts book, covered in blots and crossed-out sums. Pull up to reveal* MARIANNE *labouring over it. Her sickness has left her slightly short-sighted and she uses a pince-nez that makes her look like an owl.* ELINOR *is sewing and* MRS DASHWOOD *is snoozing.* MARGARET *goes up and looks over* MARIANNE's *shoulder. She frowns at the spider's web of ink.*

MARGARET
You'll go blind if you're not careful.

BETSY *brings in coals for the fire.* MRS DASHWOOD *rouses herself.*

MRS DASHWOOD
Is Thomas back from Exeter, Betsy?

BETSY
Yes, ma'am – he brung back two lovely fillets for you.

MRS DASHWOOD *looks nervously at* ELINOR *like a child who has been caught out.*

MRS DASHWOOD

Beef is far less expensive in Exeter, and anyway they are for Marianne.

ELINOR *laughs and rolls her eyes to heaven.* BETSY *turns on her way out to remark:*

BETSY

Sixpence a piece, Miss Dashwood. Oh, and he says Mr Ferrars is married, but I suppose you know that, ma'am.

There is a stunned silence. Everyone looks at ELINOR.

MRS DASHWOOD

Fetch Thomas to us, Betsy.

BETSY *leaves. They all sit very still.* MARGARET *is about to talk to* ELINOR *about it but* MARIANNE *stops her.* THOMAS *enters.*

THOMAS

Beg pardon, Miss Dashwood, but they was the cheapest in the market –

MRS DASHWOOD

It was a very good price, Thomas, well done. Would you be so kind as to build up the fire a little?

THOMAS (*relieved*)

Yes, ma'am.

There is a pause.

MRS DASHWOOD

Who told you that Mr Ferrars was married, Thomas?

THOMAS *builds up the fire as he answers. He tells the story with pleasure.*

———

THOMAS

I seen him myself, ma'am, and his lady too, Miss Lucy Steele as was – they were stopping in a chaise at the New London Inn. I happened to look up as I passed the chaise and I see it was Miss Steele. So I took off my hat and she enquired after you, ma'am, and all the young ladies, especially Miss Dashwood, and bid me I should give you her and Mr Ferrars's best compliments and service and how they'd be sure to send you a piece of the cake.

MRS DASHWOOD
Was Mr Ferrars in the carriage with her?

THOMAS
Yes, ma'am – I just seen him leaning back in it, but he did not look up.

ELINOR *screws up her courage.*

ELINOR
Did –

But she cannot continue. MARIANNE *glances at her compassionately and takes over.*

MARIANNE
Did Mrs Ferrars seem well?

THOMAS
Yes, Miss Marianne – she said how she was vastly contented and, since she was always a very affable young lady, I made free to wish her joy.

MRS DASHWOOD
Thank you, Thomas.

He nods and leaves, confused by the silent atmosphere. ELINOR *sits for a moment, then gets up and walks out.*

———

176 EXT. BARTON COTTAGE. GARDEN. EVE.
ELINOR *is standing by the gate, looking out.* MRS DASHWOOD *comes down the path to join her. She links arms with* ELINOR *and they stand in silence for a beat.*

> MRS DASHWOOD
> Your father once told me not to allow you to neglect yourself. Now I find that it is I who have neglected you most.

> ELINOR
> No, Mamma.

> MRS DASHWOOD
> Yes, I have. We all have. Marianne is right.

> ELINOR
> I am very good at hiding.

> MRS DASHWOOD
> Then we must observe you more closely.

A pause.

> ELINOR
> Mamma?

> MRS DASHWOOD
> Yes, my darling?

> ELINOR
> There is a painful difference between the expectation of an unpleasant event and its final certainty.

MRS DASHWOOD *squeezes* ELINOR's *arm tightly.*

177 EXT. OPEN ROAD NEAR BARTON. DAY.
A horse and cart are jogging along. The cart contains a large object tied down and covered with canvas. The DRIVER *whistles tunelessly.*

178 INT. BARTON COTTAGE. KITCHEN. DAY.

MARGARET *is standing on the kitchen table while* ELINOR *and MAR-IANNE pin a piece of material around the bottom of her skirt to lengthen it. Suddenly there is a commotion upstairs.*

> MRS DASHWOOD (V/O)
> Marianne! Marianne! Come and see what is coming!

Everyone runs out of the kitchen.

179 EXT. BARTON COTTAGE. GARDEN. DAY.

THOMAS *and the* CARTER *are carrying a small piano up the path.*

180 INT. BARTON COTTAGE. PARLOUR. DAY.

They carry the piano into the parlour and to the DASHWOODS' *joyful astonishment it fits perfectly.* MRS DASHWOOD *reads out the letter that has accompanied it.*

> MRS DASHWOOD
> 'At last I have found a small enough instrument to fit the parlour. I expect to follow it in a day or two, by which time I expect you to have learned the enclosed. Your devoted friend, Christopher Brandon.'

MRS DASHWOOD *hands* MARIANNE *the letter and a broadsheet song.*

> MARGARET
> He must like you very much, Marianne.

> MARIANNE
> It is not just for me! It is for all of us.

All the same, she looks conscious of the truth.

181 EXT. BARTON COTTAGE. GARDEN. DAY.

MARGARET *is up her tree.* ELINOR *is pulling weeds.* MRS DASHWOOD *is sitting on a stool working on* MARGARET's *dress and listening to the strains of the new song which* MARIANNE *is singing in the cottage. All of a sudden,* MRS DASHWOOD *rises, shielding her eyes with her hand. She walks down to the gate, looking out.*

> MRS DASHWOOD
> Here is Colonel Brandon! Marianne!

The piano stops. MARIANNE *comes out and they all gather at the gate to watch for the rider.*

182 EXT. OPEN COUNTRY. DAY.
Their POV *of a* HORSEMAN *in the distance.*

183 EXT. BARTON COTTAGE. GARDEN GATE. DAY.

> ELINOR
> I do not think it *is* the Colonel.

> MRS DASHWOOD
> It must be. He said he would arrive today. You must play him the new song, Marianne.

Suddenly there is a yell from MARGARET's *tree.*

> MARGARET
> Edward!

MARGARET *practically throws herself out of the tree onto the grass.*

> MARGARET
> It is Edward!

The women look at each other in complete consternation.

> MRS DASHWOOD
> Calm. We must be calm.

184 INT. BARTON COTTAGE. PARLOUR. DAY.
Tense silence reigns. Everyone tries to busy themselves. BETSY *enters.*

BETSY
Mr Ferrars for you, ma'am.

EDWARD *follows her in, looking white and agitated.*

MRS DASHWOOD (*rising*)
Edward! What a pleasure to see you.

EDWARD
Mrs Dashwood. Miss Marianne. Margaret. Miss Dashwood. I
hope I find you all well.

He bows formally to each of them, lingering on ELINOR, *who is looking
firmly at her lap. He looks anxious.*

MARIANNE
Thank you, Edward, we are all very well.

There is a pause while they all search for an appropriate remark. Finally
MARGARET *decides to have a go at polite conversation.*

MARGARET
We have been enjoying very fine weather.

MARIANNE *looks at her incredulously.*

MARGARET
Well, we have.

EDWARD
I am glad of it. The . . . the roads were very dry.

MRS DASHWOOD *decides to bite the bullet.*

MRS DASHWOOD (*giving him her hand*)
May I wish you great joy, Edward.

*He takes her hand somewhat confusedly and accepts her offer of a seat.
There is an awful silence.* MARIANNE *tries to help.*

MARIANNE
I hope you have left Mrs Ferrars well?

EDWARD
Tolerably, thank you.

There is another bone-crunching pause.

EDWARD
I –

But EDWARD *cannot seem to find any words.*

MRS DASHWOOD
Is Mrs Ferrars at the new parish?

EDWARD *looks extremely confused.*

EDWARD
No – my mother is in town.

He plucks up the courage to look at ELINOR *again and is evidently not much comforted by what he sees.*

MRS DASHWOOD
I meant to enquire after Mrs Edward Ferrars.

EDWARD *colours. He hesitates.*

EDWARD
Then you have not heard – the news – I think you mean my brother – you mean Mrs Robert Ferrars.

They all stare at him in shock.

MRS DASHWOOD
Mrs Robert Ferrars?

ELINOR *has frozen.* EDWARD *rises and goes to the window.*

EDWARD

Yes. I received a letter from Miss Steele – or Mrs Ferrars, I should say – communicating the . . . the transfer of her affections to my brother Robert. They were much thrown together in London, I believe, and . . . and in view of the change in my circumstances, I felt it only fair that Miss Steele be released from our engagement. At any rate, they were married last week and are now in Plymouth.

ELINOR *rises suddenly,* EDWARD *turns and they stand looking at one another.*

ELINOR

Then you – are not married.

EDWARD

No.

ELINOR *bursts into tears. The shock of this emotional explosion stuns everyone for a second and then* MARIANNE *makes an executive decision. Wordlessly, she takes* MARGARET's *hand and leads her and* MRS DASHWOOD *out of the room.*

185 EXT. BARTON COTTAGE. GARDEN. DAY.
The three DASHWOODS *come into the garden, still holding hands.*

186 INT. BARTON COTTAGE. PARLOUR. DAY.
ELINOR *cannot stop crying.* EDWARD *comes forward, very slowly.*

EDWARD

Elinor! I met Lucy when I was very young. Had I had an active profession, I should never have felt such an idle, foolish inclination. At Norland my behaviour was very wrong. But I convinced myself you felt only friendship for me and it was my heart alone that I was risking. I have come with no expectations. Only to profess, now that I am at liberty to do so, that my heart is and always will be yours.

ELINOR *looks at him, her face streaked with tears of released emotion, of pain and of happiness.*

187 EXT. BARTON COTTAGE. GARDEN.
MARIANNE *and* MRS DASHWOOD *are stamping about in the garden trying to keep warm.* MARGARET *has climbed into her tree-house. The branches rustle.*

MARGARET
He's sitting next to her!

MRS DASHWOOD/MARIANNE
Margaret, come down!/Is he?

MRS DASHWOOD (*scolding*)
Margaret! Will you stop –

MARIANNE

What's happening now?

MRS DASHWOOD

Marianne!

MARGARET (V/O)

He's kneeling down!

MRS DASHWOOD *can't help herself.*

MRS DASHWOOD

Oh! Is he? Oh!

She and MARIANNE *look at each other joyfully.*

188 EXT. DOWNS NEAR BARTON. DAY.
The figures of EDWARD *and* ELINOR *can be seen walking, in deep
conversation.*

189 EXT. PATH NEAR BARTON COTTAGE. DUSK.
*Later. The lovers walk slowly, their heads almost touching, their words low
and intimate.*

ELINOR

Your mother, I suppose, will hardly be less angry with Robert
for marrying Lucy.

EDWARD

The more so since she settled the money upon him so irrevocably –

ELINOR

– no doubt because she had run out of sons to disinherit.

EDWARD

Her family fluctuates at an alarming rate. Then, in London,
when you told me of the Colonel's offer, I became convinced
that *you* wanted me to marry Lucy and that – well, that you and
Colonel Brandon . . .

———

ELINOR
Me and Colonel Brandon!

EDWARD
I shall not forget attempting to thank him for making it possible
for me to marry the woman I did not love while convinced he
had designs upon the woman I did – do – love.

EDWARD *stops walking. He looks at* ELINOR *and realises he can stand it
no longer.*

EDWARD
Would you – can you – excuse me –

He takes her face in his hands and kisses her.

190 EXT. PATH TO BARTON CHURCH. DAY.
A group of VILLAGE CHILDREN *run down the hillside towards the church
waving ribbons and dressed in their Sunday best.*

191 EXT. BARTON VILLAGE CHURCH. DAY.
*A large wedding party is gathered outside the church. The entire village is
present –* CHILDREN, FARMERS, LABOURERS, SHOPKEEPERS, *and all
our* PRINCIPALS. *We see* MRS JENNINGS *in a gigantic mauve bonnet,*
CHARLOTTE *and* MR PALMER, SIR JOHN, MRS DASHWOOD,
MARGARET, THOMAS, JOHN *and* FANNY, *who is dressed in a
fantastically inappropriate concoction, and some* MEN *in regimental uniform. The path to the church is strewn with wild flowers and everyone holds
a bunch of their own. The church bells start to peal, and a great cheer goes up
as the door opens and* BETSY *comes out holding the bridal cake aloft. The
bride and groom appear:* MARIANNE, *in white lawn, and* COLONEL
BRANDON *in full uniform. Behind them come* EDWARD *in his parson's
garb and, on his arm,* ELINOR *as matron of honour.* CLOSE *on them as they
watch the party moving away.* MARIANNE *and* BRANDON *make their
way forwards, everyone throws their flowers over them, whooping and
singing.*

An open carriage decked with bridal wreaths comes to meet them, and BRANDON lifts MARIANNE in. His melancholy air is all but gone and he radiates joyful life and vigour. MARIANNE also looks extremely happy – but there is a gravity to her joy that makes her seem much older.

According to the custom of the time, BRANDON throws a large handful of sixpences into the crowd, and the VILLAGE CHILDREN jump and dive for them.

The coins spin and bounce, catching the sun like jewels. One hits FANNY in the eye. She reels and falls over backwards into a gorse bush. CAM pulls back as the wedding procession makes its glorious way from the church. We draw away into the surrounding countryside. Then we see, on the far edge of frame, very small, a MAN sitting on a white horse, watching. It is WILLOUGHBY. As we draw back further still, he slowly pulls the horse around and moves off in the opposite direction.

The DIARIES

PREAMBLE: Production meeting in Oxford Street on a raw wintry morning on Monday 15 January 1995. Lindsay Doran (producer), James Schamus (co-producer), Ang Lee (director) and I had met previously this month to discuss the latest draft of the script, which is what we're all here to work through. Tony Clarkson (locations manager) and Laurie Borg (co-producer) already know one another but this is the first time the core personnel of the shoot have met to prepare.

Lindsay goes round the table and introduces everyone – making it clear that I am present in the capacity of writer rather than actress, therefore no one has to be too nice to me. It's 9 a.m. and everyone looks a bit done in. Except Ang, who brings self-contained calm wherever he goes. Just looking at him makes me feel frazzled in comparison, as though all my hair's standing on end.

Our first point of discussion is the hunt (during which, in this version, we witness the accident that kills Mr Dashwood). Where do we get a hunt? It seems to require at least twenty-five male stunt riders – or we hire a real hunt, like the Beaufort which was used on *The Remains of the Day*. Ang wants villagers and labourers watching and to see the fox being chased. My idea is to start the film with an image of the vixen locked out of her lair which has been plugged up. Her terror as she's pursued across the country. This is a big deal. It means training a fox from birth or dressing up a dog to look like a fox. Or hiring David Attenborough, who probably knows a few foxes well enough to ask a favour. Laurie finally says it's impossible.

What Ang wants next is even more expensive: he's desperate for a kitchen scene in Norland Park (home to the Dashwoods – to be filmed at Saltram House in Devon) which would show the entire staff of Norland preparing a huge meal. I want a bleeding Mr Dashwood to be brought in through the kitchen door and laid on the table surrounded by all the raw

---

joints of meat. As Ang and I enthuse about symbolism, Laurie gently reminds us of expense. These are costly scenes and the film hasn't even started.

I look around the table and realise – perhaps for the first time – that it's actually going to happen. After five years' work on the script (albeit intermittent), the sense of released energy is palpable. There are budgets, an office and several real people here. I glaze over for a second, in shock. Pulled out of reverie by James asking, yet again, what physical activities can be found for Elinor and Marianne. Painting, sewing, embroidering, writing letters, pressing leaves, it's all depressingly girlie. Chin-ups, I suggest, but promise to think further.

We start to work through the entire script, adding, subtracting, bargaining, negotiating, trying to save money wherever we can. We get to the ballroom sequence and I suggest that we create several

vignettes that occur in the background – a rich old rake forcing his attentions on a young girl whose greedy father affects not to notice, a fat matriarch surrounded by sycophantic cousins – a Cruikshankian taste of nineteenth-century greed and hypocrisy. More expensive than simply filling the room with extras but much more interesting. Laurie's eyes roll but he agrees that it's worth the effort and money.

I have a notion that it might be nice to see Colonel Brandon tickling trout – something to draw Marianne to him. Tickling trout is a mysterious old country method of catching trout; you tickle their tummies and when they're relaxed you whip them out of the water. I ask Laurie if it's possible to get trained fish. Lindsay says this is how we know I've never produced a movie. She tells us that two of her friends had read the script and thought I'd invented the pregnancy of Brandon's family ward for shock value. It's surprising to find such events in Austen, but after all, how many people know that there's a duel in *Sense and Sensibility*? When Lindsay asked me to adapt the novel I thought that *Emma* or *Persuasion* would have been better. In fact there's more action in *S & S* than I'd remembered and its elements translate to drama very effectively.

We get to the end of the script by 3.20 p.m. and Lindsay says, 'Can we afford the movie we just described?' It's a long, complex script and the budget is pushed to the limit. James is most worried about the number of shooting days. Doesn't seem enough. (In the event, our fifty-eight days stretched to sixty-five.)

Wander out into Oxford Street slightly dazed. 'See you in April,' I say to Laurie. Now everyone goes their separate ways to continue prep. Ang and James return to New York and work on budget and schedule from there. Lindsay returns to LA to produce and I go to West Hampstead and switch the computer on. Another draft . . .

———

209

I spend the rest of January in tears and a black dressing gown.

During February and March I revise the script constantly but the basic structure remains the same. Half a dozen new drafts hit the presses but by 2 April we settle on the final shooting draft. The hunt and kitchen scenes discussed at the January production meeting have both been cut due to budget and schedule constraints.

In February, Ang, James and Lindsay return and the casting process begins. We start with Fanny. Everyone we see captures perfectly the balance of wifely concern and vicious self-interest. Ang says at the end of one day, 'This is a nation of Fannys.' It rings horribly true. Some characters are far more elusive, notably Lucy Steele and Willoughby, perhaps because of their hidden motives. Gemma Jones, Kate Winslet and Elizabeth Spriggs are so immediately Mrs Dashwood, Marianne and Mrs Jennings that we find it difficult to imagine anyone else in the roles. I'm excited about the fact that five of the actors I prevailed upon to perform a reading of an early draft last year are all hired by Ang: Hugh Grant (Edward), Robert Hardy (Sir John), Harriet Walter (Fanny), Imelda Staunton (Charlotte Palmer) and Hugh Laurie (Mr Palmer). Also that Hugh Grant, for whom I wrote Edward, has agreed to do it despite having become after *Four Weddings* the most famous man in the world. It's odd to be on the other side of the casting process. Even though Michelle Guish, the casting director, makes the circumstances as relaxed as possible, I am uncomfortably aware of how difficult it is for an actor to walk into a small room full of people staring at them. Lindsay is quite shy, James chats a bit, Ang seldom says anything at all and I make a lot of irrelevant noise whenever there's a long silence. Ang's principal criteria are unexpected. Physiognomy matters a great deal to him. Not whether a person is good-looking but the spaces between their lower lip and chin and between the bridge of the nose and forehead. Praxitelean proportions, virtually. After a first meeting with an actor there's a second during which we read scenes. I get the opportunity to play all the other roles and have a minor success with Sir John. Then a third when the scenes are put on video. Ang is not familiar with many British actors so we see people time and again until he's certain of what he wants.

'Can everyone in England act?' he says after a particularly engaging afternoon. Lindsay and I think about this one for quite some time before deciding that probably the answer is yes.

Ang presents a collection of intriguing contradictions. He does t'ai chi but his shoulders are constantly bowed, he meditates and smokes (not at the same time as far as I know), he hasn't an ounce of fat on him but eats everything going, especially buns. When I cooked roast beef for him he ate *all* the Yorkshire puddings – about eleven. He's forty years old and looks thirty.

As each role gets cast, the fact of the shoot becomes increasingly concrete. I rewrite scenes with the actors in my head. At the end of March I go away for two weeks, try to forget about the script and think about Elinor. This diary begins on the first day of rehearsals.

F R I D A Y   7   A P R I L : Shepperton Studios house the production offices and rehearsal rooms. We are working on one of the smaller stages where, last year, we filmed some interiors for *Carrington*. Rehearsals with Gemma and Kate. Both surprised to find that Ang begins with meditation and exercises – this is not usual. We sit on cushions and breathe. We massage each other's pressure points. It's very painful. Loud screams, particularly from Winslet.

I'm still doing rewrites in the evenings – small points to do with location and honing dialogue. There's always something. We're asked to do written homework for Ang. This is also unusual. he wants character studies and sets a list of questions, mostly addressing background and 'inner life'. Inner life is very important to him. Some actors react well to this, some don't. But we all do it. Imogen Stubbs (Lucy Steele) wins prize for best effort in the form of a letter to Elinor from Lucy some years after their respective marriages (see Appendices). Before casting began I remember saying to Ang that nothing mattered more than that every actor be funny. Very witty cast.

Our session with Jane Gibson (movement duenna and expert on all manners historical) is both revealing and rewarding. We learn the root and meaning of the bows and curtsies – or reverences, as Jane calls them. As you enter a room you 'cast a gladdened eye' about you. Beautiful phrase. It has boiled down over the centuries to mean a come-on. I remember my father once saying in a restaurant where I was flirting outrageously with one of the waiters, 'Stop giving that young man the glad eye.'

The bow is the gift of the head and heart. The curtsy (which is of course a bastardisation of the word 'courtesy') a lowering in status for a moment, followed by recovery. She speaks of the simplicity and grace of the time, the lack of archness. The muscularity of their physique, the strength beneath the ease of movement. She reminds us that unmarried women would not necessarily have known about the mechanics of sex. We search for a centre of gravity. Everyone suddenly feels clumsy and ungainly. As Jane says, we don't know how to behave any more.

Hugh Grant breezes in after last night's premiere of *An Awfully Big Adventure*, in Timberland boots and specs, a blue shirt. Repellently gorgeous, why did we cast him? He's much prettier than I am. It is Ang's first rehearsal with Hugh. He admits to being nervous – they both light up cigarettes. I watch, smugly non-smoking, but am soon to return to my old habit of rolling up my own.

Hugh: 'The moral of film-making in Britain is that you *will* be fucked by the weather.'

Ang says it's the only thing worrying him. His sang-froid is extra-ordinary. I think I must take up t'ai chi.

Cloudy. We shoot make-up and hair tests. My hair looks too red, Kate's make-up not quite right. We shoot more tests and solve the problems. Libby Barr, continuity (Scottish, sparky, vast collection of *outré* earrings), clanks away on an ancient typewriter. We work on with Jane Gibson. She's deliciously fierce with us. My concave chest is expanding outwards little by little.

MONDAY 10 APRIL: Writing endless additional dialogue. This is to cover entrances and exits or wherever it's necessary for background chit-chat. Difficult for actors to extemporise in nineteenth-century English. Except for Robert Hardy and Elizabeth Spriggs, who speak that way anyway.

Jane reminds us that God is in his heaven, the monarch on his throne and the pelvis firmly beneath the ribcage. Apparently rock and roll liberated the pelvis and it hasn't been the same since. We all stand about like parboiled spaghetti being straightened out. I've covered the telly up, hidden the radio and cancelled all the newspapers. Hello, 1811.

TUESDAY 11 APRIL: No one can sleep for excitement. Costume designers John Bright and Jenny Beavan wish they had three more weeks but have done truly great work. The shapes and colours are inimitable. Lindsay's already in Plymouth frantically trying to cut the script. It's still too long. The art department object to us bathing Margaret in the parlour. Apparently they always used a kitchen or bedroom in the nineteenth century. Perhaps the Dashwoods are different, I suggest, unhelpfully.

Start to pack for ten weeks.

THURSDAY 13 APRIL: Riding side-saddle is bizarre. Lesson with Debbie Kaye, who is in charge of training the actors to ride the horses and providing the carriages – everything to do with the transport of the times. It's a huge responsibility and great to find that it's a woman's. Quite unusual in this country. She put me on Small George, who was a bit skittish. The saddle has two leather protuberances. You wrap your legs around and hold on tight. Very good for the thighs. I wobble about, trying to be brave.

MONDAY 17 APRIL: Our hotel, Alston Country House in Devon, is very grand and comfortable. We're here for six weeks to shoot the entire Barton Cottage and Norland Park sections and one interior scene in Mrs Jennings's London house. I'm in the top of the building, between eaves, rain and wind howling. No duvets but old-fashioned sheets and blankets and good tomato soup. England. Hugh Grant arrives tomorrow but I've nicked the prettiest room. Very low ceiling, so can't do Reebok stepping without knocking myself out.

Kate arrived looking slightly wild. Said her solo sessions with Ang had reduced her to a squashy bit of cotton wool. She's practising the piano on a keyboard in her room.

James Schamus and family are here. I gave their small child an Easter egg. Quick dinner with them and Ang and his wife Jane who's visiting with the children for a while. We talked about her work as a microbiologist and the behaviour of the epithingalingie under the influence of cholesterol. She's fascinated by cholesterol. Says it's very beautiful: bright yellow. She says Ang is wholly uninterested. He has no idea what she does.

I check this out for myself. 'What does Jane do?' I ask.

'Science,' he says vaguely.

Laurie Borg turned up, a wild look in his eye. His girlfriend had left early because he's not interested in anything but getting *Sense and Sensibility* started. We're all at it . . . Long psychological investigations of character over dinner. Why does Morag (Ross, make-up designer) always wear black? Laurie thinks she's very spiritual. We all think Lindsay needs to work less hard. James finds the National Trust rather suspicious of us all. He's had to sign a contract – otherwise they would not have allowed us to start rigging at Saltram tomorrow. Which would mean no lights and therefore no shooting. I'm trying to adjust to new home life and family. Quite calm under circumstances. My nails and cuticles, however, are bitten to buggery.

Kate and I at dinner revert to girlieness thus: 'Oh no no no I'm not eating, oh all right just a starter then, ooh that looks good, can I taste it, give it here then, are you going to finish that? christ no of course I can't have pudding bring four spoons, just an inch then, just to relax me, no don't take the bottle away it's a waste definitely no coffee do you have decaf?' etc. It's pathetic. I'm thirty-six and ashamed of myself.

My bathroom looks like the cosmetics department at Harvey Nicks. Aromatherapy oils mostly, which I never use. Tranquillity. Harmony. Anti-depression. Quiet time. Deep relax. Anti-stress. There's a shower attachment on the bath that does not bode well. Have invested in a ghetto blaster. Bunged on Handel's *Messiah* until I got depressed.

Bed with the script, Austen's letters, a sore back and wind. Inside and out.

TUESDAY 18 APRIL: Slept like the dead. Seared mouth on very hot porridge at breakfast with Lindsay. We discussed the 'novelisation' question. This is where the studio pay someone to novelise my script and sell it as *Sense and Sensibility*. I've said if this happens I will hang myself. Revolting notion. Beyond revolting.

Lindsay said that the executive she had discussed it with had said 'as a human being I agree with you – but . . .' I laughed until my porridge was cool enough to swallow.

Good-luck flowers arrived at home from Danny de Vito and Jim Sheridan. There's class for you. My mother has filched them. Sun's out. Off to get my roots dyed. Party tonight for the cast and crew to say hello. Yacht Club in Plymouth. I have no desire whatsoever to go but it's a good idea.

Kate looks a bit white. The bravest of the brave, that girl. I can't imagine what sort of a state I would have been in at nineteen with the prospect of such a huge role in front of me. She is energised and open, realistic, intelligent and tremendous fun.

Bought herbal teas – anti-stress, relax, quiet time, deep sleep etc. Did a work-out, bent double. Somewhat foxed by my new music machine – can't work out how to rewind tape. Nineteenth century clearly encroaching faster than I think.

9.30 p.m. Back from party. Crew were rigging and didn't really show till 8.30. But we tarted about and said hello to a few folk and they all seem great. Hugh Grant arrived. Slammed into a pint of bitter and some chicken goujons like nobody's business. I had a glass of water and tried to keep my hands off the scampi.

Morag showed me an eye-shadow container she'd bought for me. 'It's cosmic,' she said. I opened the lid and lo and behold, there was an Austen quotation: 'It was a delightful visit, perfect in being much too short.' A happy coincidence. I'm tired and must to bed.

WEDNESDAY 19 APRIL: Was up at six to a peerless sky and frost. Sunken roads are beautiful to behold and Devon lambs remarkably handsome. Arrived for the opening 'Big Luck' ceremony – a Buddhist ritual Ang observes at the beginning of every film. He had set up a trestle table with large bowls of rice, two gongs, incense sticks, oranges (for luck and happiness), apples (for safe, smooth shooting), a bouquet of large red-petalled flowers (for success) and an incongruous pineapple (for prosper-

216

ity). Everyone lit a stick of incense, bowed in unison to the four corners of the compass and offered a prayer to the god of their choice. The camera was brought in on the dolly (which is a small wheeled platform on which the camera, operator and focus-puller sit) for a blessing, and a few feet of film were rolled. Ang struck the gongs, we all cheered and planted incense in the rice bowls. I cried. Al Watson, one of the electricians (or 'sparks'), passed Ang and said, 'Is this going to happen every day, guv?'

Rehearsals begin for Kate and Gemma's first scene – a difficult one to start with, very intimate and full of grief. They talk about Elinor's growing attachment to Edward and in her responses Marianne reveals her romantic sensibilities and sets up the image of her ideal man. We're also aware that behind Mrs Dashwood's equally romantic visions is a harder-edged reality – she must get her daughters married for their financial and social security. To find the balance between profound familiarity and informing the audience about character is hard. I'm very concerned not to allow ourselves any false affection – the sentimentalised 'close' family who are always caressing each other. I don't think they exist. Neither Gemma nor Kate is sentimentalist, but still, it's always something to watch out for.

Margaret's tree-house is palatial. Not quite what I had in mind. Fabulous thing. The National Trust volunteers hover, watching us all like hawks. The welcome to Saltram was not the warmest. 'This house is much older than any of you and deserves your respect.' We all feel like a group of disreputable roadies. Clearly, they expect us to lay waste to the place. It is alarming, however, to see the sheer numbers of a film crew (about one hundred and twenty people) and the weight of equipment. The expressions on the faces of the volunteers veer between a diffident shyness and nervous terror as another jack-booted bruiser comes clanking in with large bits of metal that miss the precious mouldings by a whisker.

The sparks are, however, very respectful. I notice one tall blond, unreasonably handsome in an Aryan way, and poke Al Watson between the ribs. 'Who's *that*?' I ask.

'Paul Kemp,' he says. 'Yeah, I know. It's all his own, that hair, not dyed. We tease him something rotten, poor lad.'

'Well, it's always nice to have someone beautiful to look at,' I murmur.

'Not good enough for you, am I?' says Al, who then presses some of his wife's excellent bread pudding into my grasp. Al worked on *Carrington* last year. It's a small world.

Saltram is a wonderful house – but, like all that has been preserved and not used, has an empty atmosphere. I dare say we will soon see to that . . .

Chris Newman (the first assistant director, who controls the set) and I have been on five films together (*Much Ado, Howards End, Peter's Friends, Remains of the Day* and this) and he has always looked the same. A touch of Indiana Jones, felt trilby, khaki, long blond hair, bearded, with a low, authoritative voice.

Bernie Bellew is the second assistant director, who coordinates everything from the 'base' and is responsible for getting the actors to the set on time. Base comprises actors' trailers, hair and make-up buses, catering bus, toilets, construction and electrical vehicles, generators and so forth. Looks like backstage at a fairground. Bernie is a young, gentle man with blue eyes and hair that was already greying when I first met him on *The Tall Guy* in 1988.

Ben Howarth is our third AD. Tall, with a faraway look that belies his efficiency. He chases us all up and is constantly on the move as he listens to Bernie's instructions on his earpiece.

Rebecca (Becca) Tucker, the runner, is quintessentially English-rose with a sweetness of character to match and a firm hand. Runner is a good job description – she does everything at speed.

Three scenes down. Gemma and Kate triumphed and shook a lot all over. Nerve-wracking to do the first shot on anything. Hugh and I did Edward and Elinor talking and walking and got cold. The sun shone, everyone divested themselves of puffa-jackets. Then it hailed. I wondered about the Big Luck ceremony a bit after that, but Ang seemed quite pleased to have cloud. Paparazzi arrived for Hugh. We had to stand under a tree and smile for them.

Photographer: 'Hugh, could you look less – um – '

Hugh: 'Pained?'

My first director's note (criticism) from Ang: 'Very dull.' A bit of a blow. Then: 'Don't look so old,' which didn't help. But we've started. We're off. He was cock-a-hoop by the end of the day and no wonder since there were hardly any disasters. Lots of public watching, quietly interested.

Home 8 p.m. It took me two hours to remove make-up, have bath, make calls, eat a pear and light some relaxing candles. 'Night-time' teabags and anti-stress oil in the bath. None of it works; I'm zinging.

T H U R S D A Y 2 0 A P R I L : Up 7 a.m. after a fractured night's sleep. Very cold. Found two lambs in the road, tried to get them back to their mother and failed horribly. Left them bleating ferociously at us from the middle of a bush. Porridge, toast and a large pot of tea during make-up. Sore hairpins, very long lighting job. Edward finds Elinor crying for her dead father, offers her his handkerchief and their love story commences. Ang very anxious that we think about what we want to *do*. I'm very anxious not to *do* anything and certainly not to think about it.

I've ink everywhere from practising with quills. Kate very calm and happier today, I think, now she's up and running. Indoors, thank God, all day.

219

The morning flew by with Hugh, who is as great an actor as I've always thought. So light and yet very much *felt*. He's made Edward rather troubled and halting, almost a stammerer. It's particularly good because it illustrates how relaxed he feels with Elinor, with whom he can be both funny and fluent.

Harriet (Walter) has chosen a dog for Fanny. It's pointy and shakes all the time. In her close-up we all had to wave cake at it to stop it staring into the camera or at its owner. Didn't faze Hat for one second, but the dog thought we were mad.

I've learned that Hugh and I caused Ang great suffering the other day. He has never had any actor question anything before. In Taiwan the director holds complete sway. He speaks and everyone obeys. Here, actors always ask questions and make suggestions. In this instance he'd designed a particular shot where Elinor and Edward walk through the gardens at Norland talking. Hugh and I were concerned about shooting (or 'covering') their expressions as there's so little time in which to see these people fall in love and the shot seemed too far off to capture them. In the event his idea was much better than ours, but that we should have had an idea at all came as a genuine shock and he was deeply hurt and confused. Better today, after Lindsay and James explained that these were perfectly normal working methods. We talked and I think he feels easier. I feel terrible – as though I've ruined Ang's first day by not being sensitive enough to his situation. It must have been terrifying – new actors, new crew, new country and then us sticking our oars in.

Chastening to realise yet again how much I have to learn about being too impatient and overwhelming. Bed in a heap of rubble.

FRIDAY 21 APRIL: Not much sleep. Demonised myself to such an extent last night I half expected to rise with two small horns. Wrote to Ang last night – this culture shock thing works both ways, it seems. Ang gave me a hug and said he was so touched by my letter he couldn't sleep. So we're all on course again but I am being cautious with my suggestions. I'm appalled to find that Emilie François (Margaret), who is twelve, is keen to 'lose a few kilos'. Does all that horror really start so young these days? I snorted a lot and forced a Jaffa Cake down her.

I'm freezing.

No dramas. Lindsay and James also suffering slight culture shock and a bit frustrated by the pace of things. Ang expects the ADs to be the tough ones and they expect him to be the tough one. So no one's tough and things move slowly. The beginning of a film is like watching a huge newborn centipede trying to get up on its hundred legs and go for a walk. Keeps tripping up until it's worked out how to coordinate. Any film will take two to three weeks to get into its stride – some never do. I think the key is good communications.

A care package arrived from Columbia Pictures: dressing gown, slippers, bath-pillow, blanket. A *care* package. Half expected a Zimmer frame (one of those balancing frames you get given when you're old and wobbly). Very kind. Caring, even.

Roast beef and a square of chocolate for lunch. Very yang. I keep tripping over my frock and swearing.

9 p.m. Alston Hall. Back after completing the day's work, no dramas. Terribly wound up. Adrenalin flowing. Difficult to sleep even after such long days. The hours vary – never less than twelve; today, fifteen. Ang very keen on the yin and yang of *Sense and Sensibility*. His sensibility very unsentimental, like Austen's. They're remarkably connected. She'd be astonished.

Sometimes there are eight or more National Trust volunteers in the room when we shoot, all in varying states of suspicion. The fire alarm went off. Fire engines came racing; we all rushed out on the gravel drive, everyone thinking it was us. In fact, one of the elderly residents of Saltram had left a pan on the oven in her flat. Apparently this happens all the time. The tenant in question is appearing as an extra – playing one of the cooks.

Huge spot on my cheek. Security guards for Hugh, poor soul. Ah, what it is to be a matinee idol and followed around by nutters.

SATURDAY 22 APRIL: Cannot seem to sleep these days. Woke at 1 a.m. convinced it was time to get up. Back to bed with a scowl, a plum and Her Letters. Frantic dreams once I finally slept.

The hotel clearly switches central heating on late at weekends. Freezing at 6.30 a.m. and no hot water.

10.30 a.m. Pissing down with rain and very cold, which makes everyone depressed. Bought large bag of sweets which we all sucked noisily.

SUNDAY 23 APRIL: 1 a.m. Finally about to go to bed after hugely full and successful day. We've finished this period at Saltram without having dropped (filmspeak for having failed to cover something) a scene. A couple of shots had to go, but I don't think they'll be necessary. Ang very relieved. Mick Coulter (director of photography – Glaswegian, witty, perfectionist) and Phil Sindall (camera operator – shy, sensitive, patient) are pleased. It is an extraordinary achievement on all their parts, given the exigencies of the location. We'll return here in a few days and finish the Norland section.

Woke last night and sobbed for some reason. Relief, possibly.

Harriet and Gemma delivered excellent acting every time in dining-room scene. Theatrical training . . .

Hugh Grant bought us all drinks. We sat in the bar and played daft games – Lindsay is on excellent form. Rained all day. We froze.

Woke 7.30 after five hours, wrecked. Ate all day and sat in sun. We're all bright pink. Morag will kill me. Put pyjamas into laundry after only a week's wear and felt profligate.

MONDAY 24 APRIL: New location: the front room of Mrs Jennings's London house is being shot on the Flete Estate, in the owner's home. The rest of Mrs Jennings's house will be shot in Salisbury. Most locations on film are a composite of several buildings – it's rare to find everything you need in one place, and Ang is very particular about the dimensions, colour and light in a room.

Lunchtime. Long rehearsal with Imogen Stubbs as Lucy, in the scene where Edward comes in and finds her with Elinor. There are eighteen set-ups. (Each shot is referred to as a set-up. We tend to shoot anything up to ten takes on every set-up. The number of the take is written on the clapperboard, or 'slate', and sometimes a shot will be called a slate.) It will take two days. Hugh won his Bafta for *Four Weddings* and was good in the scene. Bastard.

8.30 p.m. Home to Alston Hall. Raining. Soup, glass of wine. Very difficult scene and all a little tired but good concentration nonetheless. Four people in a room, each with entirely different motives and reactions to the same situation, requires a lot of coverage. Ang's taken to requesting what he calls 'smirks'.

'Endearing smirk, please' – which I find pretty tricky.

'Try rigorous smirk' – even trickier. I give it a go but end up going purple with the effort. Very little appetite.

TUESDAY 25 APRIL: Grey 6 a.m. We continue the scene. It's Hugh's close-up. After several takes, Ang said to Hugh, 'Now do it like a bad actor.'

Hugh: 'That was the one I just did.'

———

Ang holds his small hand to his face when anxious, a small crease on his brow.

Chris Newman turns forty. We all jeer. Corset has crushed my stomach to pulp. Studio happy with dailies (or 'rushes') – developed film which the directors, producers and sundry others watch at the end of the day. This is also rushed to the States so that all the executives responsible can check they're not throwing their money away . . . Sometimes actors watch rushes, if they're allowed by the director. Ang doesn't wish it. It makes no difference to me because I never watch them. The only time I did was on *The Fortunes of War* in 1987 – I wanted to resign, leave a note of apology and then kill myself.

I walk to work. Magic. Pheasants, cows, horizons. Fruit salad and toast, chocolate biscuit at eleven, bean and lentil curry, peas, spinach and rice, apple crumble and custard at lunch, three sandwiches at tea, no dinner – appetite clearly restored.

Hugh languid. I told him he had the stamina of a whelk. Felt we might all have done rather 'period' acting today. Most confused. But we finished the scene, a minor miracle. You don't expect to get nine set-ups in a day as each one requires a re-light. This is when the sparks take over the set and move lights about and the actors go away and gossip. It can take anything up to three hours. Mick and Phil a bit grey about the gills.

WEDNESDAY 26 APRIL: Finished at Flete with Elinor offering Edward the living at Delaford courtesy of Colonel Brandon. Very moving, the heartbreak beneath the courtesies, Edward's attempt to apologise, the great unspoken love between them. I couldn't get through the rehearsal without crying at the thought of losing someone so irrevocably . . . Did entire scene in four hours or less (five set-ups), not bad, and Hugh was great. I irritate him with all my hugs of affection but generally he's very sweet to me. Nice to be out of that room.

It's 3 p.m. and we're back at Saltram. Weather changeable so it's possible we'll do the stables scene. Everyone knackered as dailies went on till midnight. Bit peeved, they all were. The material continues to satisfy so no problems as such. Lindsay wants more emotion, Ang wants less. Hugh wants quite a bit and I don't know who I am any more. Ang slowly accustoming himself to the way we work – he says English crews are slower but that is because there's more respect and the ADs don't yell at them like they do in America. I think he likes it.

We're not allowed to touch or move any of the furniture in Saltram, which makes for amusement. Today I saw an elderly lady, one of the volunteers (who are allowed to touch the furniture), being asked whether we could move an antique bench. She pushed her handbag firmly up her shoulder, picked up the bench and tottered off on high heels, watched by six strong grips and props men all completely bemused.

Bed 9 p.m. with script. Back on schedule. Two big scenes tomorrow. Getting quite nifty with a quill these days.

THURSDAY 27 APRIL: Slept for nine hours! Time for a real breakfast. Small George (Elinor's horse) kept falling asleep under the lights in the stable and had to be poked regularly to keep his head up. Ang started to smoke in the stable, was advised against it – twice – and ran out, arms flapping, slightly bewildered.

Ang: 'In Taiwan, directors are allowed to do exactly what they want.' Then he giggled. Stood smoking in the rain and described how, in Taiwan, he would be followed about with chairs, ashtrays, wet towels, tea in constant attendance. We all stood about and looked at him and laughed.

The hotel has a wedding tonight so we're all off to another hotel in Plymouth for the night.

FRIDAY 28 APRIL: 6 a.m. call. I woke at 2.30 and had a darkish time. Nice easy scene this a.m. but I feel unattractive and talentless. I look like a horse with a permed fringe. Did poetry-reading scene where Marianne teases Edward. Ate veg and rice.

Evening in the new hotel overlooking Sainsbury's car park. Back to the twentieth century with a vengeance. Took ages to get in with key card. Hate them. I like a proper key, which must mean something. Austen very keen on keys, I seem to remember. Hugh and I wondering if we're any good. Kate seems very well. Independent soul. She's taken herself off to see *Little Women*. This hotel is unspeakably lowering.

SATURDAY 29 APRIL: Very fond of hotel. Slept like a log. Up 7.30. In to work, discussed the decision to put some of the actors in a different hotel to the rest of us, bad for morale, and also a party to be given Saturday 13th, good for morale.

Hugh G. says he finds the work very technical. I'm not quite sure what he means but I nod sympathetically. I feel the most appalling frump. Opened papers to find *The Tall Guy* and *Much Ado* advertised on the telly with casually rude remarks about them everywhere. Bit of a downer. Looking forward to some booze tonight and a decent meal with time to enjoy eating it. My body needs exercise but is holding up very well. No weight going on.

Found Ang asleep on set, folded up like a little dolly in his chair. Nice shot of Elinor and Edward walking while being watched by Fanny and Mrs Dashwood. All in one, nice and smooth. Last day at Saltram. Was going to give the National Trust boss lady a box of chocolates but I've eaten them.

SUNDAY 30 APRIL: 12.20 a.m. Soup and booze in bar. Finished at Saltram. Huzzah. Did very bad close-up at night, which didn't help my mood or fatigue, but Ang was philosophical. He

227

doesn't indulge us but is always kind when we fail. A pleasant evening. I'm lonely.

8.20 a.m. Slept heavily from one to eight. Weary but calmer from a drinking night. Bath and then a walk with Kate before lunch. Praying for good weather for the wedding. Greg Wise (Willoughby) turned up to ride, full of beans and looking gorgeous. Ruffled all our feathers a bit.

7.30 p.m. Fantastic outing, sunny drives, five courses at Gidleigh Park Hotel and skinny-dipping in the river. I'm dyeing hair with Jan (Archibald, hair designer, exceptionally good woman). Helluva week ahead. Notes from Ang for Kate have floored her but she rallies. We all got them, I remind her.

Mick's joke: What's the difference between a pig and a grip? A pig won't spend the entire night trying to get the grip to go to bed with it. He swears this only applies to American grips but it's delightfully insulting either way. Richard Broome, our grip, is a perfect gentleman as far as I can tell.

MONDAY 1 MAY: Frumpy, sad, old and weepy today. New location. Caravans miles away. Ang patient, radiating calm. Hugh has taken to calling him 'the Brute'.

Later: Everyone hauling their way through the day. Kissing Hugh was very lovely. Glad I invented it. Can't rely on Austen for a snog, that's for sure. We shoot the scene on a hump-backed bridge. Two swans float into shot as if on cue. Everyone coos.

'Get rid of them,' says Ang. 'Too romantic.'

Now on horses, which is a bugger. Sheep and all. Very bolshie 'period' sheep with horns and perms and too much wool. If they fall over, they can't get up. Someone has to help them. Can't be right. Ang wants sheep in every exterior shot and dogs in every interior shot. I've suggested we have sheep in some of the interiors as well.

Vehicles, mud, single-track roads. Impossible. Lovely weather so we are in great hopes of sun tomorrow. I feel without muscles today. Morag says we'll get through the week and bank holiday will give everyone a break.

Ang, after a particularly trying time with our flock (very quiet): 'No more sheeps. Never again sheeps.'

5.30 p.m. Very much cheerier. Just the strain of getting started again. Lovely scene on the horses, who were very well-behaved. That Debbie Kaye is a genius. Hugh and I did the first take completely out of character, we were concentrating so hard on riding and hitting our marks and not masking each other, etc. He turned into a champagne baron and I did something out of Sidney Sheldon. Got back on track afterwards but it just shows you. Gareth Wigan (Columbia executive and a great supporter of

the project) arrived – seems very pleased. Kate and I did a quick shot on a hill. I'm in and out of hats, boots, pincurls, hairpieces, the corset and different frocks every ten minutes. Bitty day. Tomorrow will be difficult and exciting and everyone is on board. Entire cast, except Imogen and Richard Lumsden.

9.10 p.m. Bed. Imelda (Staunton) down from Inverness. Alan (Rickman) also just arrived, is in the bar with Hugh G., Mick and Kate.

Incipient thrush, me. Luckily Kate had some live goat's yoghurt which I've applied with middling results. Ang told us about his early sex life today. 'So painful,' he said, then laughed a lot.

TUESDAY 2 MAY: Woke sevenish after troubled night to thick mist. Tremendous excitement at Berry Pomeroy, the exquisite village where we are to shoot the wedding. And mist. We try to convince ourselves that it's an interesting idea to do the film's last joyous shot of Marianne and Brandon's wedding in thick mist.

'It's different,' says Lindsay.

'Sort of eastern,' I add, clutching at straws.

WEDNESDAY 3 MAY: Yesterday a triumph, I think, and the most perfect weather imaginable. Mist left on cue. Found Ang having breakfast – two eggs, a kipper, a scone and some raspberry jam. 'What's so funny?' he said.

Greg on for his first day. It's like having a colt in the make-up caravan. Alan Rickman splendid in uniform. He and Kate look wonderful together.

Finished wedding. Happiness. Two cameras, ours and a steadicam (which is strapped to the body of the operator and offers more mobility), to cover the procession – much like a pantomime walk-down, actually – of Marianne and Brandon out of the church, followed by Mrs Dashwood, Margaret, Elinor and Edward (who are supposed to be already married but I can't help feeling that it will look like a double wedding. Depressing thought – too neat) . . . Mrs Jennings and Sir John, the Palmers, John and Fanny. It's Alan's first day and his last appearance in the movie. Rather confusing.

'*You* try it,' he said darkly. 'I haven't played a scene yet and I'm already married and being followed by you lot . . .'

He's suspicious about what everyone's getting up to behind his back but I assure him we're all behaving very well and trying not to go over the top. Local children appear as extras – I chat them up. They've all got names like Jacob, Saul and Abraham. Hugh G. naps on the church pews between takes. A peacock sits in the tree opposite the church and makes its mournful cry all day.

THURSDAY 4 MAY: Organising the party. Cheerier. Lisa Henson (head of production at Columbia) rang yesterday just as we were watching Greg drive the curricle (a high-flyer specially constructed for the shoot. Bright yellow with black wheels. Sexy contraption) at speed up a hill – very dangerous. We buggered the sound of the end of the shot by cheering. Odd watching that in the dying afternoon light as Lisa chatted from a morning Columbia in LA. Dailies are pleasing them – relief all round. Electronic Press Kit on set. I get very ratty. Don't like being watched by another camera. It's background material and interviews that will be used for the press later, so very necessary.

Caught sun through my costume, it's like the Bahamas. Watched all morning, didn't get on camera. Everyone in high spirits. The girls discuss the indefensible behaviour of some men who will parade their obscenely large beer bellies without a qualm and then comment brainlessly if a woman eats a bun. Make-up trailer has become very militant.

Had lunch with Alan in his trailer and talked about theatre. He was as

---

231

much put off by two years in *Les Liaisons Dangereuses* as I was by fifteen months in *Me and My Girl*. I like *evenings* too much. I'm not sure all that repetition is good for you . . .

Ang's note to Alan: 'More subtle: do more.' Alan flummoxed but only momentarily. I am constantly astounded by Ang – his taste is consummate. It sometimes takes a while to work out exactly what he wants but it's always something subtler. Try to picture myself working in Taiwan. Imagine the loneliness.

Very hot today. 9.30 p.m. and I'm off to bed. Did small scene between Elinor and Mrs Dashwood. No time, no concentration, no light and all sorts of emotional difficulty. Ang spot on with his notes – we started very hot and ended up far calmer and more flowing. Vast numbers of midges bit us and moved into Gem's wig – wind machine kept them at bay. Crows cawed like buggery – we fire a shotgun just before the take, which shuts them up for a few minutes. Who says the country is peaceful? Ang misses the motorway.

FRIDAY 5 MAY: 9 a.m. Just finished line-up for Hugh's last scene ('My heart is and always will be yours'). Peerless weather. Hugh on good form.
Ang to Hugh: 'This is your big moment. I want to see your insides.'
Hugh: 'Ah. Right-o. No pressure then . . .'
I'm slightly tense – big crying explosion to do next.

Later: Tenser than fuck now, as the morning's work only prepared me and we'll do my shots this afternoon. Make-up bus is like a sauna – it all melts off as you apply it. Went and requested air-conditioning units. Ang wanted a difficult shot this a.m. and Mick talked him out of it (he felt there wasn't enough time) and then felt a bully. It's easy to feel a terrible bully with Ang –but things are improving, I think.

———

Hugh G. has finished. He appears on set looking completely out of place in his boots and the shirt he was wearing on the first day of rehearsals.

'I'll miss you,' I say weepily.

'No, you won't,' he says.

He's quite right, of course, there's no time for all that. He walks off to say goodbye to everyone and that's the last I see of him.

10.30 p.m. Finished at 9.30 and am rewriting tomorrow's scene. It's too complicated for the time we have available to shoot it, needs simplifying.

S A T U R D A Y   6   M A Y : A very ancient lot this a.m. Lots to do but Lindsay and I cut the Thomas scene a little and smoothed out the arrival of the piano so I hope we'll get it all. Packed a bag for the weekend, determined to be off as soon as possible. The house representing Barton Cottage is also on the Flete Estate, and one of the most beautiful spots we've ever seen. Takes the curse off a six-day week.

S U N D A Y   7   M A Y : Gidleigh Park Hotel. Here for a weekend off. Walked to Dartmoor, among black-faced lambs and foals, climbed to the top of a large rock and met a small boy.

Me: Hello.

Boy: H'llo.

Me: This is a good place, isn't it?

Boy: Yes.

Me: If it weren't hazy we could see for miles.

Boy: On a clear day you can see way over to south Devon.

Pause.

Boy: That's something you can't buy.

At which point I expected him to sprout wings and ascend to heaven.

233

He was wearing a slightly disappointing AC/DC T-shirt, though, which brought me back to earth.

TUESDAY 9 MAY: Changeable weather. It was peerless at 6.30 a.m. so we got ready to do the picnic – which meant Luci (Arrighi, production designer and the most elegant woman on earth) and the art department had to change the front of the cottage to the later, lived-in look. Removing tree-house etc. took ages. Now broken clouds have arrived, which means shooting everything in both cloud and sun. This is tricky for Mick in particular. Everyone rushes in and out with polystyrene and flags, and Terry (Edland, head electrician or 'gaffer') gazes at sun through his dark glass shouting, 'Sun in about three minutes' – so we shoot a take in cloud first, and then the sun comes out halfway through and we have to stop and start again. This happens all day. Chilly. I issue direful warnings against whimsy in these love scenes. The picnic is a wonderful Luci creation. Exquisite. It looks like it's being given by the Rothschilds. I ask Luci to take away pies and cakes and fruits and all the glory. 'Cheese, bread, apples and beer,' I say. 'They're poor.'

Luci makes a plea for the pork pie. 'They could have had it in the larder,' she wails as her divine portrait is dismantled.

I am unrelenting.

We may have to hire cheaper sheep. They're not close enough for their perms to register.

4.45 p.m. Rather nippy now. Lazy picnic atmosphere. Gunshots to shut the crows up. Partridges squawk, swans fly flappily over the estuary. It's noisier than the M25. Drink tea in green room. Art department busy with the interior – glorious colours, like a Dutch painting, washed out.

9.15 p.m. Home, constipated, to a glass of water and a handful of peanuts.

WEDNESDAY 10 MAY: Weather now so changeable on all fronts that the call-sheet contains more options than a pizza menu. Different scenes proposed for the following conditions:

1. Bad weather (light wind)
2. Bad weather (strong wind)
3. Goodish weather
4. Good weather
5. Grey, still weather.

It looked like bad weather (light wind) when I rose at dawn. Checked call-sheet, which confirmed that the scene to be shot in these conditions didn't contain Elinor. Ha, I thought, and went back to sleep. Bernie rang at 8.20: 'We don't need you.' Ha, I thought and went back to sleep. Finally smoozled out at 9.45 and ordered porridge, which I ate in bed with a bit of jam. I was in heaven.

Got up and went to visit the set with Gemma. Everyone in wet-weather gear looking resigned. Mist machine extraordinary – a cylindrical contraption on a truck expelling great billowing clouds which were then pushed up the hill by the (light) wind. Nick (Wilkinson, horse-master) did stunt riding for Greg brilliantly. Big George (Willoughby's horse) is stupendous. Another specially trained horse stands in to do the rearing.

Emilie soaked to the skin and frozen all day. I gave her an aromatherapy bath afterwards. Kate rolled down the hill endlessly, happily doing all her own stunts. Rain machine. Then it *did* rain so poor crew stood about in both special effects and real rain. Everyone sodden by the end of the day and exceedingly tired. I, on other hand, had dinner and sat up talking to Alan and Gemma. A real treat.

Cannes schedule for *Carrington* (which will open at the Festival) looks

---

punishing so I'm trying to get it changed. Bit too much on, really. Or at least for me – I can't concentrate on more than one thing at a time. Bed at midnight after lots of wine but it doesn't matter because I have a day off tomorrow – incredible.

FRIDAY 12 MAY: Bernie rang at 7.30 a.m. Sun's out. Got to work. Omigod. Stare at wine-sodden eyes in mirror and hate myself.

Willoughby arrives with Marianne. Ang said the rehearsal was too hectic – and that he's been bitten by scenes like this before. So busy that the audience just switches off. He's very interesting on the flow of energy in a film. Always thinks of everything in its widest context.

Wild a.m. trying to work out the blocking. Kate and Greg sopping wet and brave. Set up a shot that was designed only to go to a certain point in the scene but as Ang didn't cut we just carried on. At the end of the scene

236

Phil said the lens was too pushed to contain anything but Ang said he'd just been watching the story – and he hadn't cut simply because he'd been enjoying himself. 'Try not to get into the habit,' said Linds, worrying about film stock and costs. Later, Ang said that he wanted the camera to watch the *room*, sense the change in it that a man, that sex, had brought. For Ang, the house is as important a character as the women.

Bed knackered at 10 p.m. Very wet people. Very cold. Cannes looking threatened. A good day, really – but there's so much to do. Paranoid delusions and loneliness struck at me so I must wise up and get to bed earlier.

SATURDAY 13 MAY: Up 6 a.m. to cloudless sky. Walked to work. Jan tells me I have to go to Cannes – she was very clear about it. I'll regret it if I don't, even if it wrecks me.

Alan R., who has clepped himself Colonel Weathercover ('weather-cover' means interior scenes that are slated to be shot if the weather is not right for the scheduled exterior scenes) and spent days on end trying to amuse himself in the hotel, is in to work finally and looking a tad bewildered. 'I'm not as well as I would like to be,' he responded to my enquiry.

Greg very energetic this morning.

Morag: 'Nothing that a syringe of horse sedative won't cure.'

Overheard later:

Kate: 'Oh God, my knickers have gone up my arse.'

Alan: 'Ah. Feminine mystique strikes again.'

Sun went in and out all day so again we had to cover the scene in shine and cloud. Alan had a trying morning – trotting up, dismounting, tying up the bloody horse, dealing with his crop, taking his hat off and reverencing on the side of a hill. Horse kept moving around so its great black arse overwhelmed the shot. Deb Kaye lay on the grass, hissing at it,

---

237

'Get back, you bastard' etc. Not Alan's happiest moment but he was splendid, charming and virile.

Lots of argument about Willoughby's arrival. Should it all be on a master (i.e. one shot only)? The crew want coverage. Ang thinks coverage is irrelevant. Should Willoughby help Marianne into the carriage, or Brandon, or both? Should Marianne say, 'Now I shall really be able to play for you, Willoughby' or is it too rude and should she address it to the whole group? In the meantime, Greg has to drive in a carriage with two horses, make them stop on a pre-arranged mark, hold them steady while acting and getting Kate into her seat and then move them off as if he did such things every day of his life. Also the horses have taken to letting off lengthy and noisome farts during the takes. Debbie says it's the Devon oats. Privately I decide to lay off the porridge. Deb's as embarrassed for the horses as if they were her own children.

Kate tells me her first note from Ang was, 'You'll get better.' I shrieked.

It's raining now. The weather reports are all contradictory and none describes with any accuracy the weather we've got. Greg and Kate in the high-flyer were a wonderful sight – genuinely transported with excitement. Probably because it's quite dangerous.

We've yet to pick up the beginning of the scene in cloud. Given up now and have come inside to do at least one set-up on the hair-cutting scene with Gemma (where Willoughby begs a lock of hair from Marianne). Sat chilled, looking at the swans and cormorants flying over the estuary. We've flattened all the grass on the lawn and it has to be fluffed up for the shot. Hilarity reigns. I feel tired and out of it and beg not to do the scene tonight. But we have to do the scene – schedule is biting. I play the scene tired and out of it. Ang likes it.

SUNDAY 14 MAY: 6 p.m. We await tea. There is a special weekend of 'miniature bear making' going on in the hotel. Appar-

---

ently a group of ladies meet regularly for nice swims, meals, conversation and a shared interest in miniature bear making. Still trying to get my mind round it.

The party on Saturday was wild. Everyone fell on the opportunity to let go and was drunk before having drunk anything. Alan nearly killed me, whirling me about the place. Everyone was under the table by midnight except Greg, who was on the ceiling. I discussed the film industry with some of the drivers – who've seen it all, of course, and get very depressed about the fact that we don't finance nearly enough films in Britain. This film was financed in the States and most of the revenue will end up there. Ridiculous state of affairs. Had a bop with Ang. Very good dancer. 'I haven't done this for years,' he said, looking surprised and bouncing about like a piece of India rubber.

Home at 3.30 a.m. in a taxi, arseholed. I stumbled into my bedroom where Harriet Walter (who'd come down specially and was sharing my room) was already asleep. She sat bolt upright.

'Help me!' I wailed.

'Oh, God,' she said. 'Why don't you try throwing up?'

A good line in that cut-glass accent, I thought, even as I threw myself at the loo bowl.

Ang's latest note to Greg: 'Great acting. I think.'

MONDAY 15 MAY: Everyone looking slightly bushed. Up 6 a.m., looked at the sky, couldn't decide what it was going to do, so washed and went back to bed. Bernie rang and told me to stay in bed, then rang back twenty minutes later and said, 'Come in.' It's sunny, finally.

Alan R. in slight state of shock about working methods but I have assured him it works. We seem to feel our way into the shots. Ang's style of leadership is somehow to draw us all to him silently and wait for things to happen. He has the shape of shots in his head always and will stand for silent minutes on end thinking through the flow of the scenes to see if what we're doing will fit his vision. I find it very inspiring but it's quite different to being told what to do. More collaborative. I think he's enjoying our ideas more now he knows they don't present a threat or a lack of respect.

5.30 p.m. Going outside to catch the last of the daylight for Willoughby and Brandon's meeting, then coming back in for Alan's close-up. Strange to have Alan and Robert Hardy on board now, it feels like a new movie. Hugh's section seems months ago and another life. There are so many different story lines in this script and we've been entirely focused on Elinor and Edward. Now Brandon's story begins. Robert Hardy brings the nineteenth century with him, he's born out of his time. Courteous, intelligent and witty in tweed. I very much like the fact that there are four generations represented in this film – from Margaret's twelve-year-old perspective through Elinor and Marianne's twenties and Mrs Dashwood's forties to Mrs Jennings's sixties. Not a thirty-something in sight.

Ang massaged my stupid neck (stiff as wood from dancing too long). Taking a long time to get up to speed today.

TUESDAY 16 MAY: 10 a.m. At last the weather's broken! Couldn't sleep last night so I'm very grateful not to be on camera today. Up at nine to do a workout, eat porridge despite fear of flatulence and join them in the rain.

Later: Lots of very cold, wet people in real rain, effects rain and mist again. Slow start. Laurie's pulling his hair out.

Ang's gentle flow doesn't seem so gentle when you're frozen but all's well. Good humour prevails. I am in very fetching white wet-weather trousers and wellies. Look as if I work in a chicken factory. This was the day a very sodden Greg bounded up to Alan and asked, with all his usual ebullience, how he was. Long pause as Alan surveyed him through half-closed eyes from beneath a huge golfing umbrella. Then – 'I'm dry.' Sometimes Alan reminds me of the owl in Beatrix Potter's *Squirrel Nutkin*. If you took too many liberties with him I'm sure he'd have your tail off in a trice.

10.20 p.m. In bed with a herbal cushion from Kate. She fainted at 6 p.m. – so cold, so wet for so long. Alan found Ang sitting on a box, his head low, his fists clenched.

'I tortured her,' he moaned.

'Don't worry,' said Alan. 'You'll have the opportunity to do it to me soon.'

Kate was sent flowers by the production and four bottles of Newcastle

241

Brown Ale from the ADs. We warmed her up slowly in her caravan, her feet thrust into Greg's armpits. According to Paul (our paramedic) this is the best way of warming feet and she made a very good recovery. The hotel had built an enormous fire which we sat around with a glass.

Robert Hardy had had the day off and found an entrancing post office in Yealmpton that he could barely tear himself away from. 'A proper English post office smelling of dust and jam with a little old lady who enquired after my health.'

Elizabeth Spriggs has arrived. Full of energy, pouring out affection like a particularly comforting teapot.

Bad weather means more rain work for Kate tomorrow so we'll have to be very careful. We sat today in a strange, tiny hut on the beach, drying her stockings before a real fire, and steaming gently. Good work today, though. Willoughby's entrance through the mist on a white horse. We all swooned. Ang laughed at us.

'This scene is ridiculous,' he said.

'It's a girl thing,' Lindsay and I replied.

Really wet, though, that rain.

WEDNESDAY 17 MAY: Up 5.45 – looked at sky. Couldn't work it out. Washed. Walked to work. They cancelled me. Came home. Went back to bed at 7 a.m. and slept till ten – out like a light. Off to the set now, to watch Robert Hardy, who looks like a caterpillar in his costume.

Later found Ang looking at the estuary with a mournful expression. I went and stood beside him. After a moment he said, waving towards the water, 'Tide goes in, tide goes out, tide goes in, tide goes out – and still no sex.'

'Do you miss it?' I enquired, after I'd stopped laughing.

He nodded sadly. His family won't be back for weeks.

Kate got rained on again. She's been a total hero and heartbreaking on the hill with the sonnet. Alan arrived and had to run up a very steep hill in thick tweeds and thermals. Then he had to stand in rain which was blinding today. Thank God we had wind and clouds.

THURSDAY 18 MAY: Managed to pee on most of my underwear this morning (trailer loos are very cramped) so I'm in a very bad temper. Didn't sleep. Had three breakfasts to make up for it. Sun is out. Amazing that the cloud held just for those two days.

Robert and Liz come down to rehearse their arrival scene. Wonderful as they can extemporise within the period. Quick rewrite on arrival scene and we've got the line in about camphor being good for 'the staggers' so I'm pleased.

1.30 p.m. Good morning. Six horses, three carriages, six dogs, six

actors – madness. All waiting for cloud. Thank God for Liz and Robert who are not only brilliant but stalwart. My bowels are up to no good today. There would appear to be several more scenes on the call-sheet. Help. Poor Emilie had a headache and a maths test today. It's hell being twelve. This week has flown. Some fight starting up over a Jaffa Cake in make-up.

7 p.m. Still shooting. Alan and Greg swanned in after a fabulous day visiting an English winery and pubs. We all spat at them. The sun has come out so we'll work indoors and go outside later. Rehearsing poetry-reading scene also.

8 p.m. Am slightly hysterical now. Huge spot has appeared on chin.

10.30 p.m. Finally in bed – far too late.

FRIDAY 19 MAY: Woke 3.30. Well and truly bollocksed.

10 a.m. Already have a couple of things in the can, shot outside in the sun. Rain came on and we moved indoors.

Ang had a go on a horse. 'This is easy,' he said as it walked very sedately along, being led by Deb. *Sense and Sensibility* signs litter Devon – arrows with *S & S* on. Whenever Ang sees a B & B sign he thinks it's for another movie.

We're working on the second scene between Willoughby and Marianne where they read the sonnet together. Difficult to give poetry reading a sexy hue in this day and age but what else can he do? Give her a massage? Must avoid twee. Oh, please don't let any of it be twee, I'll die. I'll be assassinated by the Jane Austen Society (who rang James's company in New York to complain about the casting of Hugh Grant as Edward – too good-looking apparently).

My spot has gone volcanic and I'm very bitter about it.

6 p.m. Found myself, on the turnaround of the poetry-reading scene, acting my bit while tiptoeing about among mike leads, climbing over

---

Chris (Gurney, boom operator, very stoic individual), putting props down on plastic beer boxes and picking up others, squeezing myself in beside the polystyrene and thinking, What the hell am I doing? I dare say a spot of alienation's good for you.

We all started singing 'Kumbaya' this p.m., which shows how tired we were – no one had the strength to put an end to it.

I received a wonderful invitation from a local couple with a very enjoyable sentence which ran thus: 'In particular there would be no question of anyone being advised of your being entertained here as this part of the country is famous for shellfish.'

Gemma (*to me as I scribble*): 'I do hope this diary isn't going to be libellous.'

Gemma is magic. She looks so innocent and pure and then she opens her mouth and says something rude. She's got the dirtiest laugh I've ever heard. Lindsay came into the green room the other day and asked her if she'd like a bun.

'I'd like a bun almost as much as I'd like a man,' she replied, unblinkingly.

Can't get my lenses in and grope blindly about the set.

SATURDAY 20 MAY: Cannes. Get on plane 9 a.m. – apparently it belongs to Chris de Burgh. My spot has made a third appearance and practically has features of its own. I try to improve my appearance and just end up getting a quantity of mascara in my hair. Press ahead.

7 p.m. Cannes rather quiet. They have less money from the government this year, I'm told. Pamela Anderson causing great excitement in black leather get-up. Went for a walk despite earnest pleas from the publicity folk not to: 'You'll be bothered by photographers and public,' they intone. Trotted off down the Croisette and no one took a blind bit of

245

notice except one young person who clutched her companion and hissed, 'Is that Sharon Stone?' I was thrilled until I realised she was referring to the woman behind me (who didn't look like Sharon Stone either). Charming journos all day. Foreign.

SUNDAY 21 MAY: Bad press conference on balance – useless questions and we weren't as entertaining as we might have been – but everything else went according to plan.

    2 a.m. Finally in bed. The MTV party is opposite my hotel on beach so I'm buggered. Wax earplugs and pills the only answer. What a day. Screening went very well and Chris Hampton was pleased so everyone's happy. Didn't drink too much. Was got at by the fashion police for wearing jeans on the Marches of the Palais. I had no idea there was a dress code . . . Came home to an appalling review in *Variety*.

MONDAY 22 MAY: Up early to leave. Walked out of my bedroom to find my fat face outside every bedroom door on the Cannes *Newsletter*. A surreal and essentially unpleasant moment.

TUESDAY 23 MAY: Bizarre to be back at Alston Hall. French press on *Carrington* very good. English press mixed but a good response in general and Polygram are very pleased. Press conference yielded the usual crop of daftness. I've been asked if I related personally to Carrington's tortured relationship with sex and replied that no, not really, I'd had a very pleasant time since I was fifteen. This elicited very disapproving copy from the Brits. They're like a pack of maiden aunts sometimes – slingbacks clacking and knitting needles pointing. No wonder people think we don't *have* sex in England.

    Very fine rehearsal. Beautiful day. Stiff neck. Going great on atlas-arriving sequence. Emilie has a natural quick intelligence that informs every movement – she creates spontaneity in all of us just by being there. Generally a marvellous piece of direction from Ang, who loves the unspoken undercurrents everywhere.

We had to wait a lot for wind. It blew our skirts and aprons, and the coats hanging in the doorway. Something nostalgic, lonely about it.

WEDNESDAY 24 MAY: Asleep by eleven with the help of a pill, up at six to cloud, no idea what we're doing, it changes by the moment. Fruit, toast, coffee. Ang has an upset stomach and has stopped eating pink iced buns for breakfast. His colon is grumbling. We talk about what he wants to do next. He longs for something masculine – opium wars, we suggest. Lots of men and guns.

Lunchtime. Kate and Gemma are sitting in their corsets talking about the Hollywood Porn Awards – they've found pictures of this ceremony in an old magazine. We've still not shot the master (the set-up that captures an entire scene or a large part of it. Then you cover the scene in close-up, two-shots and so forth).

Gemma, after two hours' waiting: 'Oh, God, it's like childbirth. You go on and on and on and on and still nothing happens.'

Twoish. Exhausted now and I get dizzy spells because my blood pressure has plummeted. Somewhat demoralised to have achieved only one shot by this hour. Everyone's yawning. A nine-hour break is really insufficient, but we generally get ten or twelve. This does not apply to many of the crew, though – de-rigging or prep for the next day's work can mean they get eight or nine hours off at most. The tired mood is right for this scene, though. Sun's out now so everyone's running around with filters, screens and heavy frowns. Very hard going today.

9.30 p.m. We didn't quite get to Gem's last shot, which upset her. Very frustrating after such a long wait. The ADs sent a bottle of champagne to the hotel in apology. She doesn't drink so we nicked it.

247

THURSDAY 25 MAY: Slept well for the first time in days and without pills. Bits and bobs today and wholly reliant on weather. Picking up this and that as we can, rather confusing. A sheep collapsed from heat exhaustion. Just keeled over in the back of shot. The shepherd's worrying about his flock and is always asking when he can shear them. After this we told him to go ahead. They appear later, with haircuts, behind Marianne and Margaret as they walk.

FRIDAY 26 MAY: Lovely relaxed evening last night, clouds scudding across sky. An odd day, with a confusing number of scenes, plus doctors and acupuncturists for my neck and Mick's back. Everyone went in and out of the green room as various consultations took place. Plus a fair bit of snoozing. Rain. Winding down, mellow atmosphere. It will be like starting yet another movie next week. Am munching ham sandwiches. Robert Hardy left a crate of champagne. We live for pleasure. I've done nothing but eat all day. Morag said I was getting thin in the face. Fell asleep in Kate's lap. Feel very calm. Odd. Ang still off the buns and the smokes. We need some sun.

Later: Ang sitting shredding a polystyrene cup with a little frown creasing his smooth brow. Second unit are doing carriage run-bys (shots on moving carriages with no artists, although Roy Bond, one of the drivers, is standing in for Mrs Jennings. He's the same shape but has a large moustache. It won't read). All the girls from hair and make-up are doing tapestries. It started with one or two but has spread like wildfire – they're all at it now. Most peculiar.

Lindsay comes in with the silhouette scene typed up. I think it's good. We need more dialogue for Sir John and Mrs Jennings as they walk up the path. Ironically that's one of the bits I cut down as it was almost three pages. I remember, back in the mists of pre-production, saying, 'They'll do it very quickly,' which cut no ice at the time.

Kate makes a bracelet. We're in our nighties, our plaits down our backs. Ang settles down for a snooze. The weather does worry him. Only one day left at this location. Hypnotic, Kate's hands knotting the threads.

Shrieks of laughter ooze up from downstairs. Ang asks about theatre – how anyone can do eight shows a week for months on end. Nightmare visions of *Me and My Girl* hove into left-hand side of brain. Thank God there's no tap-dancing in this film. The green room full of biscuits, buns and half-eaten sarnies, plus Monday's newspapers. Ang under such enormous pressure I'm surprised his colon hasn't crawled out of his mouth, never mind grumbling. Discussion about shots and us (Kate and I) sometimes looking less than perfect. Ang says, that's not what it's about, looking good. We agree, fervently. Typical mid-term reactions settling in – Paul the medic rushing about supplying vitamins, laxatives, herbal sleeping pills, aspirin and God knows what else.

Said goodbye to everyone at Alston Hall this a.m., which made us sad. I was so relaxed there I took to removing my make-up in the bar, sitting cross-legged in socks and leaving little damp pads of cotton wool everywhere. Disgusting, when you come to think of it. The staff looked after us like family.

We try to find an extra line for Margaret as she picks up Willoughby's gear in the rain. Lindsay suggests, 'I'll get the stuff,' which makes me laugh immoderately.

I counter with Willoughby saying, 'Pray get the stuff.'

'It's in the book!' we keep screaming.

Lindsay is having a horrid time of it. There's so much left to shoot. She's made a list of 'luxury' scenes and 'crucial' scenes. We almost didn't shoot Elinor listening to Marianne packing and deciding not to tell her about Lucy's engagement. Did it in the end, hoping it will be effective in one shot. Tempers fray. Candles are difficult to work with.

SATURDAY 27 MAY: Up 5.15 a.m. thinking, packpackpack. I appear to have accumulated more things. How does this happen? I haven't shopped. Think my bath oils have bred.

It's raining and dull and exactly the sort of weather we don't need. Will reshoot the Dashwoods' reaction to Edward's arrival ('I do not think it is Colonel Brandon') in the rain. Will it match the interior? Probably not. This is where Mick works magic and creates false sunlight. His concentration is terrific.

Ang must be getting better. He produced a lot of Chinese snacks for us last night – crunchy peas and freeze-dried cuttlefish.

Fell asleep at lunch and awoke to find Emilie, Kate, Ang and Greg playing games. It's not like work at all today. I'm *not* working, of course, but it doesn't feel as if anyone else is either. Ribald laughter floating up from the garden where the sparks are clearing away. Raining. Cosy.

Shooting Willoughby carrying Marianne up the path. They did it four times. 'Faster,' said Ang. They do it twice more. 'Don't pant so much,' said Ang. Greg, to his great credit, didn't scream. The image of the man carrying the woman is horribly effective. Male strength – the desire to be cradled again? Had sage discussion with John Jordan (focus puller, very gentle) over the barrel of the lens about allowing all those politically incorrect desires their head. I'd love someone to pick me up and carry me off. Frightening. Lindsay assures me I'd start to fidget after a while. She's such a comfort.

My roll-ups keep going out. Kate makes hers like small sleeping bags. It's impossible to imagine not leaving this place a mass of polystyrene cups and cables. But we will. The art department has added so much in the way of lintels, outside and in, shelves, plastering etc. that it's not easy to picture how it will look in its civilian state.

The estuary very Turneresque today. Soft air. Doing wild tracks for sound now – we all sit quietly as Tony Dawe (sound recordist, merry, keeps hens) records atmosphere and the odd line or two that we haven't managed to get 'clean' during the take.

Ang must be getting better. He's eating pickled cucumbers out of a tin.

TUESDAY 30 MAY: Weekend in London. Tea, mooching, Chinese food; fought my way through the garden and then the mail. Travelled Monday with Kate and Imelda to Yeovil and found myself in a glory of stone and wisteria at Montacute – the location for Cleveland, home to the Palmers. The move of location has energised the troops, although a weekend always leaves people looking shell-shocked. We're five and a half weeks in with six and a half to go. The time shoots by. I determine to savour every precious moment daily and of course in the very nature of it there's almost no time to savour anything.

Talked about the long Brandon confession scene with Alan. The trick is to break up the bulk of the information with character and to make it a scene about – as Alan puts it – a man thawing out after having been in a fridge for twenty years. The movement of blood and warmth back into unaccustomed veins is extremely painful. The scene has existed in many different forms – flashbacks, stylised imagery – until I realised it was emotionally more interesting to let Brandon tell the story himself and find it difficult.

We're already juggling with the weather as it's going to improve and we need to do the exterior shots at Cleveland in grey at least.

4 p.m. Back to hotel (which is a glorious place called Summer Lodge in Evershot) after having done nothing but rehearse a little, dye my roots with Jan and eat. The Cleveland section of the story is fragmented anyway – and our days will reflect that.

WEDNESDAY 31 MAY: Glorious sunshine. Hugh Laurie has arrived, which is a great fillip. There is no one on the planet who could capture Mr Palmer's disenchantment and redemption so perfectly, and make it so funny. He's writing a novel in between takes, in his trailer.

We prepare to do, 'I think Marianne may need a doctor.' Hugh surprised to learn that it's at night. 'Have you read the script?' I enquired tartly. Recalled Hugh Grant's words – 'I'm never acting with the screenwriter again.'

It's true I'm always at them. The language in the novel is complex and far more arcane than in the later books. In simplifying it I've tried to retain the elegance and wit of the original and it's necessarily more exacting than modern speech.

Spoke to Christopher Hampton, who's very pleased about *Carrington* and tells me it's doing great business in France.

Three interior scenes today. Thank God we did Friday's work yesterday – weather seems set to improve. Spoke to Stephen Fry, who sounds very cheerful and is driving back across the States. Once, last year, my computer scrambled the script and because I am a computer-illiterate fool, I had no back-up. No one from Apple Mac could rescue it so I took it over to Stephen's and he spent an entire day finding it. I hyperventilated with gratitude for weeks.

Tourist saw Alan and said, 'Oh, look, there's Tom Cruise.' Probably the same one who thought I was Sharon Stone.

9.30 a.m. Still not shooting. Late start again. They refused to let us use the breakfast room yesterday so we re-set the scene of waiting for Dr Harris's diagnosis in a great hall, which changed the nature of the scene entirely. Quite good really, because it's tenser. It's perhaps better for suspense that the Palmers are more nervous than I've suggested in the script.

Mick's lighting for me coming downstairs with a candle was very complex. Tried the false candle with wires and batteries strapped in a bum-bag round my waist, the switch for it trapped between the cheeks of my arse, and realised it wasn't going to work. Hugh L. had his first spoken syllable and got very anxious. It's very hard starting one's part in the middle of a shoot. Kate and I are on so consistently that we've forgotten the camera's there. Best thing.

National Trust very strict with their hours – but very nice people who actually seem quite pleased to see us.

Ang is in heaven. There is no dialogue. 'This is pure cinema,' he says, pleased.

I seem finally to have stopped worrying about Elinor, and age. She seems now to be perfectly normal – about twenty-five, a witty control freak. I like her but I can see how she would drive you mad. She's just the sort of person you'd want to get drunk, just to make her giggling and silly.

Ang is thrilled with all the topiary in the gardens. He had Marianne walking by this extraordinary wiggly hedge. Apparently it snowed one year and the snow froze the hedge. When the thaw came, they cut away the dead bits and continued to grow the hedge – in the shape of a wild snowdrift. It looks like a brain. 'Sensibility,' said Ang, pointing to it triumphantly. 'And sense,' he continued, pointing in the other direction towards a very neat line of carefully trimmed flowerpot-shaped bushes. The stone and lines of Montacute – grand, almost too grand though they are – give this part of the story a Gothic and mysterious flavour.

The public visit, casting curious glances and smiling shyly but making no enquiries or requests. Medieval oak-panelled rooms and very good-looking cows. I'm hungry. Hugh L. and I still regretting the frankly disastrous cream tea we scarfed yesterday.

Bad news. Big George died at 3 a.m. yesterday. Debbie is in a terrible state. She loves them so and he was a remarkable horse. Enshrined forever, I hope, as one of the most romantic quadrupeds who ever lived. Greg very upset too. We made tea and Deb told us the story – a ruptured colon. Very quick, mercifully, and totally unexpected, nothing could be done. Grave news and we try to cheer ourselves with thoughts on his film credit and flowers.

Now we set up a very complex shot on Alan entering with a very wet Kate, the Palmers and Elinor rushing to him and between them carrying Marianne off and leaving Brandon standing exhausted in the middle of the hall. Ang wants to do it all in one shot so it will develop from a two-shot on Brandon and Marianne into a single shot on Marianne into a four-shot on Charlotte, Mr Palmer, Marianne and Elinor and back into a single shot on Alan. It's going to be difficult and superb, I hope, if it works. Huge numbers of people watching and a lot of Chinese press.

Everyone very excited by this shot. It's so different to the style we've had to use in dialogue scenes where there's far less movement. Put on my costume. Barrier against the twentieth century. Funny how alien they feel at first and how safe and full of history they become surprisingly quickly.

Ang, on returning from a restaurant: 'The acting in England is much better than the food.'

THURSDAY 1 JUNE: The worst news. Christopher Reeve (with whom I worked on *The Remains of the Day*) has been badly hurt in a riding accident. Black, black day.

Sense and Sensibility is about love and money. Perhaps its main question is, can love survive without money? A pithy question. Romantic codes teach us that love conquers all. Elinor disagrees. You need a decent wage, a competence. Some people need more. Some people need more money than love. Most people would rather have love with a comfortable amount of money. It's a difficult thing to accept. It cries out against all our cherished ideals. But interesting that our 'western' romantic symbols cost a great deal. Roses, diamonds . . .

The lawn is covered in daisies, which indicate the wrong season. Chris Newman asks all the members of the public who are watching to pick them off. Wonderful image as they all kneel obligingly and get to work.

Journalists on set. One informed me she'd seen *Carrington* in Cannes and didn't like it. 'Oh,' I said.

I'm so exhausted today that any extra demands make me tetchy. Must stop smoking. My one roll-up idea develops into five or six and it's madness.

Harriet Walter and James Fleet are back, commenting on the real oddness of having been away so long. I felt like that on *Remains* – missed everyone terribly and wanted to work more. It's a great privilege to be completely involved from start to finish.

Dinner with everyone, which nearly killed me. Staggered into bed at 11.20 and woke with the light at six. Glorious light.

FRIDAY 2 JUNE: A bugger of a day as it's sunny and there are four huge windows, which makes lighting the room exceptionally difficult – and we've a crying-baby shot in every scene. Ang furrowed, hand against his cheek, all morning. So much to do. Much tension. Mick never wanted to shoot here because of the windows. It's supposed to be wild and stormy – what if the sun shines all day? We'll have to build platforms and create the weather outside each separate window. Impossible in the time. We were lucky. It clouded over.

Thinking up lots of additional dialogue keeps me busy. We've hired the calmest babies in the world to play the hysterical Thomas. One did finally start to cry but stopped every time Chris yelled 'Action'.

Later: Babies smiled all afternoon. Buddhist babies. They didn't cry once. We, however, were all in tears by 5 p.m. Very fractious. By 8 p.m. we were all in an antechamber telling stories to keep ourselves awake.

SATURDAY 3 JUNE: Bed with a pill at eleven. Woken at three by the birds, at four by the draught and at six by the light. In to work with a stiff neck for 8 a.m. Pissing down. Perfect. Must finish early as the move to Salisbury will kill everyone. Haven't had enough sleep this week and next week is night shoots. I'll look ninety.

Imelda (*to me*): 'You'd suit a bad perm.'

Very nice lady served us drinks in hotel and was followed in by a cat. We all crooned at it. Alan to cat (*very low and meaning it*): 'Fuck off.' The nice lady didn't turn a hair. The cat looked slightly embarrassed but stayed.

SUNDAY 4 JUNE: 8.40 p.m. State of shock as we arrive in Southampton to ghastly modern hotel on a roundabout. After our protected, countryfied existence it's a rude awakening. I am melancholy. Tomorrow a gigantic day so am putting self to bed severely early.

MONDAY 5 JUNE: 6.40 a.m. Grey skies. Slept so well I'm a new man. And that's unusual. Will cloud burn off?

8 a.m. We're about to do line-up for a scene that's thirty shots, two cameras and almost the entire cast. Very seriously overstretched. One can feel everyone's sinews tautening.

9.30 a.m. Make-up and hair full of people going from pillar to post. A line-up of staggering complexity. Lots of folk from the *Much Ado* crew have joined to do Camera B. Still can't work out weather. Morag relieved to find I'd slept. I'd started to look exhausted. Must be disciplined this week.

The curtains in this new hotel are very efficient so the light didn't wake me at four. I like it here.

Ang looks rested and says there's a decent Chinese in Southampton. Phil, he and Mick very anxious about the amount we've got to do. Hugh Laurie felt the line 'Don't palm all your abuses' was possibly too rude. 'It's in the book,' I said. He didn't hit me.

Lunch. We've managed the Louma crane (from which the camera, sans operator, is suspended) shot and that's all. Didn't turn over till 11.30. Period cows with balletic horns. Excitement. Today's work will have to be completed in two weeks' time. It was always impossible to get this in a day and we can't shift the night shoots which start tomorrow, willy-nilly.

9 p.m. Just back. Think I'm allergic to horses. Did about six shots out of the thirty. Two set-ups on the Louma crane, two on Camera B and a dolly shot on Camera A which brought Nick very dramatically in on a wonderful horse, scattering period cows. Imogen had a radio mike taped inside her parasol so the angles she held it at became rather crucial. Lots of standing about. I smoked too much. We've much more to do but what we got was divine. Mrs J's hat figured largely.

TUESDAY 6 JUNE: Night shoots. 7 p.m. Wilton – the home to the Earl of Pembroke – is our location for the interiors of the ballroom sequence where Willoughby encounters Marianne and makes it clear that their relationship is over. It's a breathtaking place. Camera crew already tense about the size of the rooms and the difficulty of shooting anything in them, let alone with a crowd of extras.

9 p.m. Waiting to dress. Tension mounts. No time to rehearse. It's dark. Think I'm getting conjunctivitis. Saveloys for breakfast. A hundred extras in evening dress, every one differently characterised, from soldiers and lawyers to fops and dowagers. A monumental effort on the part of costumes, hair and make-up. Lindsay is bowled over by it. Dancers rehearse and candles are lit in rooms full of ancient and exquisite

paintings. I've lost weight and my evening dress feels loose. Pulled boobs up as far as they'd go but they're still disappointing.

Midnight. Completed first shot. Liz Spriggs on fine form as the engine of the scene. The interiors are extraordinary and we're so agog there's no problem in playing the awed Misses D. up from the country.

3 a.m. Sewn back into costume after a spot of veg curry which is already playing havoc with my colon. Rather tense line-up for Robert Ferrars (Richard Lumsden) being introduced. Of course it's very sparsely written on purpose as I didn't want to lengthen script with unnecessary introductions, but now it feels rather bald. I'm adding things, and trying not to panic.

Jane Gibson (movement teacher) is back. I stand up as straight as I can. She fixes me with a beady eye: 'Don't slump.'

We've done the antechamber and are moving into the ices room, which is full of beautiful syllabubs and sorbets made of icing sugar. A million

different problems need to be addressed and everyone's point of view is necessary for the scene to work, which means shooting it from each character's angle of vision. With eight or nine characters present and not enough time to shoot everyone singly, the first problem is to work out where to put everyone so that we can include two or three people in a single shot. Then you have to avoid 'crossing the line'. This is a mysterious business. It's up to the director of photography, operator, director and continuity person to keep tabs on 'the line'. If you cross it the effect can be disastrous – people are looking in the wrong direction, essentially, so the screen grammar goes to pot. Where 'the line' is from moment to moment is sometimes so complex that I've known continuity people who've been in the business for decades to scratch their heads and take a long time to work out where the actor should look in relation to the camera.

A small knot of people gather in the middle of the room and scratch their heads. Even I've started to clamp my hand to my cheek. Ang's has been glued to his for hours. Also on night shoots each person's low point comes at a different moment so eyelids droop from 1.30 a.m. onwards at varying intervals. Smoke too. This is produced from a little canister and wafted about the room. It diffuses the light and is very effective on camera but it eats up the oxygen. Kate felt sick and then wanted to cry. She can't afford to, it takes too long to re-do the make-up. I do Jimmy Cagney impressions to distract her. She asks me to go away. My Uncle George is playing an extra in a powdered wig. Alan Rickman sent a huge quantity of chocolate to keep us all going.

WEDNESDAY 7 JUNE: Back to hotel by 9 a.m. Shoved a fig into my face and went to bed. Woke at 1.40 p.m. for a pee and a moan, went back to sleep till five. Quick shower and back to base for make-up. Drops from local doctor (a dish, incidentally) for incipient eye infection. Very sore. Paul the medic run off his feet. Kate's foot has swollen – inexplicably.

Immensely thrilling line-up with all the dancers and musicians. One camera on a platform and one on the dolly. Managed first dolly shot and top shot by elevenish. Stuart Hopps is brilliant with his choreography. He seems to be able to teach it without saying anything. The ballroom looks wonderful. Huge fire. Lights hidden in false pillars and then an incongruous collection of Mick's paper lanterns hanging from the painted ceiling to light us. Met Henry Herbert (Earl of Pembroke), a charming man who's just worked with Ismail (Merchant) and is still reeling. Tried to remember the dance steps I'd learned six weeks previously, dropped my stole and tripped up every single dancer in the set. No real food or drink allowed in these rooms on pain of death so this looks like the teetotallers' ball. I'm hoping the audience will assume eating and drinking goes on elsewhere, mainly in the ices room.

Elinor bumping into Willoughby feels good and exciting, especially coming out of the comedy between her and Robert. I had never imagined this scene occurring in so many different rooms but Ang's vision is full of movement – and notions of class. He's put Willoughby's party into yet another room – even more elite than the rest – so when Marianne sees the portrait of wealth surrounding him the message is crushingly clear. Kate probably won't get on camera tonight but is staying up anyway to remain on a similar time scale. The combination of heat, smoke and airlessness affects eyes and energy.

THURSDAY 8 JUNE: Kate's got phlebitis in her leg and a limp; my eyes are pinker than Ang's breakfast buns. Home this a.m. at 7.30. The boys had a beer. Bed eightish – restless but I must have slept till four, because I had a dream about Betty Bacall. Also about laughing. One rarely dreams about laughing. Interesting. Pat Doyle's

261

fault probably. He's the composer. Scottish. One of a family of about thirteen so the effort to get noticed in a crowd has never worn off. He makes me laugh almost more than any human being I know.

It's raining, which makes everything much more difficult and damp. Everyone gets wet travelling between base and the set, so make-up and hair are run off their feet. The dailies, Lindsay says, are fantastic.

Scrambled eggs for breakfast at 6 p.m. Don't eat much through the night. Even the extras are having a good time, they say. Ang munched illegal bread on set and giggled. He's happy, I think. Troublesome rehearsals but I hope all will be well.

Kate came down stone stairs very carefully in order to protect her leg, slipped and hurt her wrist. She's at the hospital now having an X-ray. Frankly, I'm not expecting her to survive the night.

I had a glass of water in the Earl of Pembroke's sitting room, which is the size of a field. My eyes have decided to recover a bit and nobody's cried yet so we must be doing well.

Miss Grey (Lone Vidahl) arrives. She's gorgeous. Much better-looking than any of us, and that includes Paul Kemp. Everyone stares.

Kate is back. It is just a sprain. Bandages everywhere.

FRIDAY 9 JUNE: Slept from 6 a.m. to 3.20 p.m. We're unexpectedly well ahead and will be able to go back for pick-ups in the ices room. Huge tax bill arrived so somehow I've got to get to a bank. Hugh L. kept treading on the train of Imelda's dress, which pulled it down so far it exposed her boobs. Keep it in, I said, but she wouldn't. Fed up with breakfasts. Caterers grey with fatigue.

SATURDAY 10 JUNE: Champagne on wrap: a gift from Ang to the crew. We must've woken the Herberts up squealing. Marvellous week. James Fleet did his close-up last at 6 a.m. and made everyone laugh so much he got a round of applause. Subtle mobility of his face bewitchingly funny. I could watch him for hours.

SUNDAY 11 JUNE: Drank far too much last night and woke at 5.30 a.m. Could've gone on drinking all night. Quite grateful for a hangover, it provides a bit of peace. Walked on to my balcony completely naked last night and took the couple that have moved into the suite next door slightly by surprise. Walked back in calmly affecting insouciance and then bit all my pillows, one after the other.

MONDAY 12 JUNE: Back to Trafalgar to shoot interior scenes in Sir John and Mrs Jennings's drawing room at Barton Park. Lucy reveals to Elinor her engagement to Edward. Two days' work and lots of acting. Imogen a wonderful combination of coy and calculating. Kate's phlebitis much better and my eyes clear.
    12.45 p.m. First shot of day. Robert Hardy extemporised a wonderful story for Margaret as they play with the map. Spontaneous applause from crew. Late finish 8.20.

TUESDAY 13 JUNE: Took a full thirty seconds to work out where I was this morning. Fried eggs and Florentines have produced a spot. Very painful morning – five and a half pages of dialogue with seven actors involves a lot of clever footwork. We all play the scene amid a welter of flags and lamp-stands trying to provide eye lines as the crew go cross-eyed trying to avoid crossing the line, which would appear, in this scene, to be in fifteen different places at once. It all goes something like this: Ang works out what he wants the actors to do. The actors keep saying, 'I wouldn't do that – I'd do this.' Specifically, I say, 'If I've just heard the man I love is engaged to someone else, I'd sink into the chair behind me, not one halfway across the room.' So things get changed, agreed to and the actors go off to make-up. Then the camera crew say, 'I can't shoot this' or 'We can't light this', and everything gets changed again. Then the actors come back and say, 'I can't do this', so it all gets changed again. We don't finish the scene. Lindsay looks for another profession. Mick swears that Ang swore when they first visited the location that there would be only two shots involving the windows. Ang has changed his mind. Mick looks for a different profession. Lindsay and I are upset about two paintings that seem very out of place in Sir John's house but which Ang is devoted to. Also we complain about the size of the room, which doesn't seem big enough to 'take a turn' in. Ang looks for a different profession. 'It's murder,' says Mick, but his cold sore is better.

WEDNESDAY 14 JUNE: New location: Mompesson House in Salisbury. We are using it for Mrs Jennings's London house – all exterior scenes, plus the drawing-room, bedroom, hall and breakfast-room scenes. The Lucy-meets-Edward scene has already been shot in Devon. There are only eleven people allowed in any room at one time. I understand the structure needs protection but why eleven? A volunteer stands outside counting and calls out at intervals, 'Could someone leave, please?' They're not keen on us at all.

I got four hours' sleep. Wired, after doing the difficult bit of the Lucy scene last (of course).

Base camp has been set up in the car park of Salisbury Cathedral. Kate and I walk through the cathedral grounds to Mompesson. Hardly anyone gives our bonnets and empire lines a second glance.

Liver and bacon for lunch after three short scenes all covered in single shots in the bedroom. Good swift work.

———

Lovely fax from Sydney Pollack (executive producer) saying how much he's enjoying dailies. He's extraordinary – working like Hercules on his own film, *Sabrina*, but always finding time to watch our stuff and comment regularly. I'm glad he likes it. During the early stages of the scriptwriting it was he who asked the most useful questions.

'I'm from Indiana,' he said; 'if I get it, everyone gets it.' He wanted to know why Elinor and Marianne couldn't just go out and get a job. Why was Edward so dependent on his mother, why he keeps his promise to Lucy when he clearly no longer loves her. Why Elinor keeps her promise to Lucy and does not reveal the engagement even to Marianne. The probity of these people is difficult to accept sometimes – but it is balanced with behaviour of quite the opposite kind from Fanny, Lucy and Willoughby. Elinor and Edward seem both to belong to the eighteenth century, the age of Augustan reason. They are firm, balanced, judgemental, drily humorous, far more Alexander Pope than Walter Scott. Marianne shoots towards the middle of the nineteenth century, embracing each romantic ideal like a new lover. The turn of a century seems always to produce a Janus-like generation, some clinging to old systems, some welcoming the new age. Always a powerful time. As for 1995, hm. Difficult times. Everything more confused than ever for women. Haven't got the strength to think about it.

Back at Trafalgar, we're doing a carriage scene on a low-loader. This is a vehicle upon which is slung the carriage and the camera together so when it moves, the carriage seems to move. Five more scenes to do today. Kate and I are zombies, smoking, crunching peppermints and drinking water. Only achieved one take in the low-loader – it takes so long to set up. Added difficulty of finding a stretch of country road free from modern articles. Ang rode off on a bicycle and didn't return. Found him locked in the loo at Trafalgar, having broken the key. He's being rescued at present.

6.30 p.m. after tea and toast. Still waiting to do our side of the carriage

---

shot. Ang said today, 'Only three more weeks.' I said I was planning a breakdown. He nodded and said, 'The blues – for two weeks, I think.' Most films take a week of the blues to recover from, he says; this one will take two. I was rather flattered. Seriously, though, I feel I shall never be the same again.

THURSDAY 15 JUNE: Kate did her breakdown scene wonderfully well. In nearly all the weepy scenes I've tried to get one good joke. Less indulgent.

FRIDAY 16 JUNE: Doing Elinor's 'What do you know of my heart?' Why did I write a scene with so many words in? Endless. But Mick, Ang and Phil worked through it merrily enough and we managed not to cross the line.

I've hardly noticed Salisbury but it is exquisite. We sit like a cricket team on the green outside Mompesson. Taramasalata for breakfast. James Schamus is back. Said he rang Columbia's distribution arm and got our executive's secretary, who said, 'Sense or What?' He'd never heard of us or it.

The set infested with tapestries, little circles of women, sewing. Very eighteenth century.

Interesting and difficult scene this – getting the level of Elinor's explosion just right. The level of control. I rely entirely on Ang – I can't quite get outside it. Pleased so far and hope I can hit it again this p.m. Barely able to eat, stomach knotted. We shoot largely out of sequence, of course – so I've already done the loss of control in the last scene, which I tried to make as involuntary as possible. A case of the diaphragm taking over. I remembered going to the bank shortly after my father died to try and sort through his papers. I was feeling perfectly calm and sat in the office talking to the manager when suddenly my diaphragm lurched into action and I was unable to do anything but sob helplessly. Walked home, shoulders heaving, thinking, This is weird, because I couldn't stop, there was no possibility of controlling it. It's never happened before or since and was as though the emotion was quite disconnected from actual thought. That was what I wanted to duplicate for the scene when Elinor finds out Edward isn't married. *This* moment, though, is much more one of anger – which I've always found very difficult. It's a hotness that's hard to simulate, a sharp heat. She's furious with Marianne but hates feeling the anger and doesn't know quite what to do with it. Like watching someone trying to bottle a genie. In the event I play it several different ways so that during the editing Ang has plenty of choices. He won't know what the right note is until he sees it in context. This is the real bugger with film – sometimes you cannot tell where to pitch an emotion and the only safe course is to offer up as many alternatives as possible.

S A T U R D A Y   1 7   J U N E : Hung over again. Got up this morning and could not find my glasses. Finally had to seek assistance. Kate found them inside a flower arrangement. Bags under my eyes purple.

Suddenly realised that for five years, every time I've finished a job I've gone back to rewrite this script. This will be the first time I can actually stop. Take it all in.

Weather dull and we're all a trifle confused because the scene numbers keep changing. Hugh and Greg are playing the blues on their guitars.

Raining, of course, so I am doing bastard close-ups on camera with the hangover from hell. Fine but weary and giggly. Later in my trailer, the boys are in to watch the rugby – wild with excitement and very apologetic. South Africa *v*. France. Apparently it's very important. Telly dodgy so Hugh has to hold it above his head at a 45-degree angle. They take turns to watch and yell. Tremendous business, sport, really. I wish I

267

could get that worked up about it. Do you have to grow up with it? The boys' faces lit up with pleasure and excitement, it's really very inspiring, she said, sounding a hundred and four.

SUNDAY 18 JUNE: Watched *Blind Date* and picked my feet.

MONDAY 19 JUNE: Delaford picnic scene outside at Trafalgar. Ang delighted with a large pile of Melton Mowbray pork pies which he calls pork buns. A holiday atmosphere in this wonderful weather but we are really up against it. Schedule changed again today as we desperately try to cram all the remaining material into the Salisbury section. Ten weeks have gone – hard to believe I'll be home on Sunday. Finished picnic. Huzzah. Now we move indoors to do the scene where Brandon watches Marianne making a silhouette of Willoughby. Very hard to light but Willoughby's profile behind the screen is effectively erotic.

I wasn't hungry at lunchtime and am now reduced to eating leftover mince from someone's plate and fudge. People have started to talk about the wrap party. Christ. Two and a half weeks yet and a lot of big scenes so I'm in no mood for count-down. Maybe we'll have a live band . . . Chinese food? Thinks.

TUESDAY 20 JUNE: Much to do. Tension. The sun yesterday produced vicious red welts on everyone, like jellyfish stings. Most sinister, I thought. Bed with a roll-up, a beer and a sleeping pill last night. Not the happiest combination.

Did 'intolerable woman' very quickly at 9.15 a.m. and continued p.m. into Brandon's first entrance. Strain telling on me today. Pronounced around the eyes so of course we did a stills session. Ha.

The day of a thousand shots. Gemma fainted twice. Affected by fumes from the generator, we think, plus corsets, heat and airlessness. Paul had to give her fifteen minutes' oxygen the second time. Terrifying. Ang hanging in rags. I've got low blood pressure and cystitis. Excellent.

Alan was very moving. He's played Machiavellian types so effectively that it's a thrill to see him expose the extraordinary sweetness in his nature. Sad, vulnerable but weighty presence. Brandon is, I suppose, the real hero of this piece but he has to grow on the audience as he grows on Marianne. Making the male characters effective was one of the biggest problems. In the novel, Edward and Brandon are quite shadowy and absent for long periods. We had to work hard to keep them present even when they're offscreen. Willoughby is really the only male who springs out in three dimensions (a precursor to her other charm-merchants, Frank Churchill in *Emma*, Wickham in *Pride and Prejudice* and Henry Crawford in *Mansfield Park*).

WEDNESDAY 21 JUNE: Fitful sleep. So many scenes, so many words. Kept waking with them all trudging about in my brain. It is, of course, very cloudy as we need sun and have no more weather cover for this location. We are trying to do the 'Mr F' dining-room scene in a single morning. Chris thinks the impossibility of it will speed things up.

Gemma a bit fragile today but better.

Bleached moustache.

Ten set-ups achieved in four hours. Lay down at lunchtime and was pronounced clinically dead by most of the ADs. Sun has come out, so we're on to the second half of the Delaford picnic scene. Triumph.

Threw Laurie Borg in swimming pool after unit still (photograph of cast and entire crew). Much satisfaction all round. Being production manager is no fun. Bed 9.30.

Woken at midnight by fucking Morris dancers outside. It's midsummer's night, and they're giving it hop on the roundabout outside the pub. I know it's a marvellous tradition and all that but it seems to lose a great deal in translation. Didn't there used to be something *Pagan* about it? Looks like something John Major designed. Damn them for waking me.

THURSDAY 22 JUNE: Back in Salisbury car park with many horses, and extras for the scene outside Mrs J's house. Still can't believe what we achieved yesterday. Beauteous day on the village green, just grand. Takes ages to re-set everyone, so getting lines wrong becomes hugely bad news. A gaggle of schoolchildren come and watch. Mompesson sits there like an etching.

Noon. Finish scene with Alan.

Me: 'Oh! I've just ovulated.'

Alan (*long pause*): 'Thank you for that.'

James says it looks as if we have the carriage gridlock scene back. It's been a hostage to time and budget all the way through but it is very important to Ang. He also said that the extra energy required from everyone at present to get the scenes done just makes them better. I whirled on him. 'Don't say that!' I wailed. It makes you feel the rest of it has been under par.

Ate a lunch that consisted almost entirely of fat and had to lie down, comatose.

Very crowded today, and hundreds of spectators on the green, who are very well-behaved and seemingly interested in watching a bunch of men in shorts carrying lamps about and laying cables. Humans are rather enchanting sometimes. I get into present-giving mode, which is worrisome. Need the filming to stop so I can go shopping . . .

FRIDAY 23 JUNE: Everything moving at wild pace so that we can get to the Brandon confession scene first thing tomorrow. Rather bracing

---

and good. Tension gone. Mrs Jennings's parrot makes its first appearance. It's an English parrot, George. Vicious beak action. There's something intrinsically funny about a parrot. They have a baleful air that suggests that nothing you did could ever impress them.

I wrote a new line for Liz: 'Ah, Pooter. Still alive, I see,' which she delivered impeccably.

Ang's family is back. He looks very happy. Tide has presumably come in and stayed in. Script meeting at lunchtime on the big Brandon scene. Home soon. Ma says all my plants are dead.

We sit on the green and eat ice cream in the afternoon, watched by the curious. There's a school sports day on by the car park and a most unexpectedly rally of Morgan sports cars in the cathedral grounds. And a film crew on the green . . . English life roaming on in a very E. M. Forster fashion all about us. John Major has threatened to resign. Perhaps to devote more time to Morris dancing? It's the first bit of news I've heard for months. Realise how entirely I have been living in this world.

8 p.m. Dye roots with Jan.

SATURDAY 24 JUNE: Alarm startled me deeply. Was in a dream about mushroom soup. 9.30 a.m. and I'm still dreaming. A good calm feel and start to the day. Wonderful to have Alan, in whom one can so trust. We tried to create a space in which he can move at will, so this scene has its own life and we don't interfere too much.

The story of Brandon, Eliza and Beth is really like a penny dreadful but Alan manages to bring such a depth of pain to it – and it's shocking within this world suddenly to hear of pregnancy and early death and betrayal. Lindsay drove in with me and spoke of her worries concerning the love stories – so little time to set them up. Really the sisters' lovers spend so much time off screen – and neither is ever seen acting *like* a lover.

271

Prevented by circumstance – so it's all implication. Very difficult balance to strike – for then one has to accept Elinor's pain about losing Edward so much later. The balance will very much lie in the editing, of course. It's frightening to think we might have *enough* of Edward and Brandon and Willoughby. At least we know that over the years we've tried everything – bringing Edward back in the middle (which didn't work as there was nothing for him to do), seeing Brandon and Willoughby fight the duel (which only seemed to subtract from the mystery), bringing Willoughby back at the end: a wonderful scene in the novel which unfortunately interfered too much with the Brandon love story. I wrote hundreds of different versions and it was in and out of the script like the hokey-cokey.

Everyone reacts variously to leaving location and going home. It's both a relief and a strain after all this time. It means the family unit is split up as everyone returns to their usual homes and routines. It is bizarre how film units become large extended families in which everyone has a role. You know whom to go to for what. Roll-ups from Sid, bread pudding from Al, a hug from Mick, wit and wisdom from Lindsay, calm from Ang, female philosophy from Morag, sound advice from Jan – and to some extent this disintegrates when people go home and resume their genuine family roles. There's a sadness to finishing on location, therefore. But of course the only reason we assume these roles is because we miss familial comfort and affection. Once home, many people become more relaxed. It's a strange balance, this life.

Lindsay appears in her maid's outfit. She's appearing as a servant in this scene. I take her through curtsying. She begs not to have to speak. We're going to make her. They're still lighting. A big master and then coverage. Trying to avoid windows. Didn't start shooting till 11.30. There'll be mutiny if we're not out by six as everyone is exhausted and there's only one day off and three different London locations on Monday. Did first bit of scene. Ang distinctly underwhelmed by me.

A very grumpy crew worked on till 8.45. Alan brilliant. Goodbye, Salisbury. Goodbye, location. Hello, London.

SUNDAY 25 AND MONDAY 26 JUNE: A weekend! At home. Not on camera on Monday and took day off. Felt guilty. Crooned over plants. Cooked a meal. Trailed round house picking things up and putting them down again. Couldn't settle to anything.

TUESDAY 27 JUNE: Greenwich. Strange to be at large in London. Traffic and spectators all over the place.

Intensely irritating day – people everywhere, Film '95 (TV show), *Premiere* magazine interview and endless personal visits which, although pleasant, are hard to fit into the scheme of things. It's alarming to discover how insular you become making a film. Strangers on set can make me feel quite savage sometimes. I don't know why – protectiveness, possibly? Personal dramas everywhere. Very hot. Coffee-shop scene with Harriet, Richard and James – they were wonderful. I rushed about correcting posture of extras, making a nuisance of myself and smelling. Hugh G. in a spot of bother up LA, apparently. Something to do with a blow job. It's all right for some, I thought.

WEDNESDAY 28 JUNE: Little sleep. Left early to watch line-up with Tom Wilkinson (Mr Dashwood) and Gem. The first scene of the movie, therefore vital, and I wanted to be there. Tom has watched a lot of people die and spoke of their detachment. Very true.

Day off otherwise. Saw Chris Hampton, who was testing explosions for *The Secret Agent* (his next film). He wants the biggest one (surprise).

Now we wait – they've had to remove a wall because the action takes place both in the room and in the corridor leading to it and the camera needs more space to contain it. It's good we're in studio for everyone's tired and it is of course easier to control the space and light. All in good spirits, though, and Shepperton feels busy.

Hugh G. is all over the papers – who attack with typically hypocritical glee and are enjoying themselves horribly. Have written to him.

Shepperton dressing rooms slightly ropy. Old pube-infested soap in bathroom and no towels. I've got a telephone, which is a great luxury, and a view of some cars, some corrugated iron and some scaffolding. Very London.

Me (after six hours' waiting for line-up): 'I'm off. I hate waiting when I'm not working.'

Lindsay: 'Most women wait. I just found a way to make a living out of it . . .'

Gem: 'She had very big lips, that hooker . . . Bet it was a good blow job.'

Boiling heat.

THURSDAY 29 JUNE: Still boiling. Decided to have Dr Harris bleed Marianne. Adds to edge. Shepperton shimmering in the heat. Difficult to sustain this tense mood. Kate's drained by playing illness. Very great build-up to 'do not leave me alone'. I shall be very glad when it's over. Reached shot 500. According to tradition, champagne (courtesy of Lindsay) was served – at lunch, so none of us could drink it.

Felt bleak about losing Morag for the last week (she goes on, with Alan, to do *Michael Collins*). But Sallie (Jaye, make-up artiste and genuine wit) will do me and we'll laugh a lot. She says she is planning a few changes. Possibly a beard.

Very shaky today. Long wait after lunch for Colonel Brandon's 'What can I do?' scene. Nice shot but a tense affair. Long chat about the line

'Barton is but eight hours away', which made me tetchy. Ang said that logically and given the light in the shots, this would be too long a journey.

'It's been in the script for years,' I snapped, unhelpfully. 'Couldn't we have had this conversation in 1993?'

Lindsay was very calm and solved it brilliantly, I thought, with 'Barton is but a day from Cleveland'.

Consumed vast numbers of sandwiches and sweated freely.

FRIDAY 30 JUNE: 8 a.m. already stocious in make-up. We're shooting the near-death of Marianne today. Premenstrual tension strikes me and the temperature is going to be in the mid-90s. No air conditioning in the studio. Horrible feeling of constriction in chest and unable to sit or be still. Longing for the scene to be over.

9.30 a.m. Still lighting. I pace and contemplate Elinor's rigidity and how to play this version of her loss of control. Terrifying for her. Did waking-up scene and the whispered 'Elinor' from Marianne. My stiff neck came in very useful. Dr Harris bleeding her adds about three hours to the day. Ang has got excited about the shot. Elinor carries a bowl of her sister's blood into the darkness. It will take forever to light. But it's close to midday and three set-ups left to do. Sitting cross-legged against the radiator thinking about swimming in very blue salty water. Think I must try not to cry but it might be difficult. Waiting for lighting. Like waiting for the tumbril. Or an exam. The sun outside and construction noise make me feel inexpressibly melancholy. Frightened, too.

5.15 p.m. That's the close shot over with. Interesting, as it all came out very vulnerable and scared. A child begging. Much better, I think, than adult held-in sobs. I hope it was the right way. Very little I can do about it now. Ang says he's never seen me in such a bad mood. 'It's like trying to talk to a bear,' he said. All over now and I'm back to normal.

SATURDAY 1 JULY: Put back out. Old injury from *Me and My Girl* days. Lumbar region goes into spasm. Fuck. Fuckity fuck.

SUNDAY 2 JULY: Carriage gridlock scene. This is a scene that Ang has always wanted passionately – where we see Mrs Jennings, Lucy, Elinor and Marianne arriving at the ballroom (the interiors of which we've already shot at Wilton). He wanted to see a jam of carriages – so many that they have to alight quite far from the entrance and pick their way through the mud and horse dung to the door. Evening. Pissing down.

Tried to deal with back. Acupuncture, frozen spinach, Indocid (a muscle-relaxant) and wailing. Am falling apart. Presents from Harriet, James and Liz. It really is finishing. Rather tearful, the lot of us. Pleased it's raining – it suggests ballroom will be steaming and smell of wet wool.

For reasons known only to themselves, the caterers did a Spanish evening – paella. This will be a wonderful shot and then it's bed with my back drugs. I smoke in an empty trailer. The papers full of Liz and Hugh in a most revolting and upsetting way. Was reading Dennis Potter's last interview with Melvyn Bragg. He said he'd like to shoot Rupert Murdoch. He can't now, but I could. In the absence of an ashtray I sit flicking my ash on to the carpet. I am a slut.

MONDAY 3 JULY: New location in Rotherhithe. Church scene. ('They always kneel.') Iced back. Slept well. Started to write farewell cards, which is making me cry. Threw minor tantrum in make-up bus, which was sans kettle, and shrieked that there was a week of major scenes to do and it's not over yet.

Hanging about waiting for the carriage mock-up to arrive (a false interior constructed on a low-loader so we can just shoot through the windows). It's stuck on Tower Bridge. Debbie Kaye said that last night's

---

scene was the biggest done with horses and carriages in the UK for twenty years. I sit in empty trailer drinking tea, smoking, tending to back. Feel like getting in a taxi and going away for a week's lie-down. Grey cold day in the East End.

The journey through London fascinating. You forget what a vast farrago it is and how ancient. I lead, I am reminded, a sheltered life in North London – a remark I made about my mother to her face when I was seventeen. Why she didn't thump me I'll never know.

Back exercises. Hobble about geriatically and beg for sympathy. No one cares. They're making a film. Feeling very emotional. Hardly a surprise; this journey – or this bit of it, at any rate – coming to an end is unthinkable and amazing. I will carry on, of course, with Lindsay, Ang, James and Pat Doyle and all the postproduction folk. But so many leave us – Mick, Phil, the fantastic camera department. A bunch of nicer men you could not hope to find. Losing Morag already was hard. Waving goodbye to each of the actors in turn is always difficult. O Christ. Drink a lot of water. Lie down. Shut up.

We've been waiting three hours now – for two bits of wood on a trailer. Kate's on loo talking to me. She's lost her Columbia dressing gown. Yvonne (our dresser – and a fabulous rock-and-roll singer) says she knows this one's mine 'because there's a large food stain down the front'.

6.30 p.m. I've finished my bit and have gone to look at the tenements. These do not, of course, appear in the book but we're experimenting with a new point of view – Brandon's as he comes to find his missing ward. It might be interesting to see a moment's worth of the pain and misery Austen refused to dwell on. On the other hand it might destroy some kind of unity. No idea. Pat Doyle is appearing, with cold sores and a dog.

TUESDAY 4 JULY: Shepperton. About to do my entrance shot. Sal suggested a nice blue eye shadow. I managed to talk her out of it. Very difficult scene for Gem just now, who was saintly about it. I was irritating and interfered.

Home nineish. Acupuncture.

WEDNESDAY 5 JULY: Back hurts. Lots to do. Did eleven takes – the family scenes are so much more difficult to capture than the emotional stuff. Primary emotions like anger, fear and sorrow, even happiness, are a doddle in comparison with an exchange of dialogue that makes Elinor and Marianne, for instance, genuinely appear to be sisters. An ordinariness, a familiarity that is profoundly elusive. No acting, actually, is what it amounts to. Turning round, then we move on to the bedroom scene, which I pray to God we finish. I think I've written all my cards. It's worse than Christmas.

After lunch I'm in rags (my hair) and I feel I should do the rest of the day in a Southern American accent. At present confined to quarters producing prop letters with a quill for the close-up writing shots. Good not to be in a corset.

Already 5 p.m. and three shots to go. Difficult to get right – an odd mixture of teasing and serious. I'm concentrating too hard on Kate and her bits and being rather bad in my own. Mick lighting away for my close-up. I keep wandering backwards and forwards shouting, 'Ready!' Drives him mad.

Weather's turned out nice and I'm having a roll-up. Started to smoke it outside but Becca told me my nightie was see-through so I've had to come back in.

THURSDAY 6 JULY: Kate and I inadvertently drank too much so I was up at five. Wrapping bloody presents. Mother's birthday. I cut a peculiarly loud rose from front garden and shoved it through her door.

Back better. Feels less fragile. Lindsay in to say that the scene with Gemma was not lit to Mick's liking and we'll have to shoot it again. Oo-er. Kate and I in right old state doing 'Dearest Papa' – frightening and too emotional, at least for this old bag. Too much emotion slopping about anyway, never mind playing scenes about dead fathers and dying sisters. Kate was calling up some tears and I whispered, 'This will be over soon and we'll be parted.' We immediately both burst into loud sobs. Having a widdle and a roll-up to recover. Hot in that studio – good grief.

Last shot on Oliver Ford-Davies (Dr Harris) to complete deathbed sequence and then moving on to tenements which I'm not in. Phil had a go at preventing my escape. 'Oh, I think you should be there – as writer,' he said, twinkling.

'Fuck off,' I replied, elegantly.

Wrap has begun with the arrival of an amazing eighteenth-century cushion from Mr Rickman.

FRIDAY 7 JULY: Last day of shoot. Driving in to Shepperton at 6.30 a.m. squashed into the back of the car with all the presents and a unicycle between my knees (it's for Bernie, who, contrary to appearances, is a wild thing). Very successful morning doing Christmas. Ang very moving – loved his tea caddy but would have been happy with a teabag. Hugged me for a long time in silence. Everyone weepy.

Sun's come out. I lie down and listen to sounds of construction. We're all down at Kempton Park Racecourse now. Hot. Picnicky and fun.

Last shot for me was at 7.30 p.m. Slate 549. In the carriage. Alan's got Wimbledon on. I didn't even know it *was* Wimbledon. It's the women's final. I cast aside my sweat-soaked corset in some relief while Kate collapses on the grass. She cries. I beg for alcohol.

10.15 p.m. Off home. Finished on Take 5 of Slate 550. A shot of Alan cantering against the sunset. The camera is inside a large gyroscopic white sphere, hung off the end of a small crane attached to a truck. Quite by accident I got a place on the back of the truck and witnessed the final take of the shoot go down, followed by the sun. Then we ate hamburgers and rubbery chips and drank champagne and there was much love around. People very moved. Lindsay and Laurie cried. I just grinned from ear to ear all evening. All within Elinor's breast was strong, silent satisfaction (it's in the book).

SUNDAY 9 JULY : Real life kicks in. Weird. Fantastic wrap party. Ang gave a Chinese banquet. We sang to him. He spoke to me for some time about the joy of his job. For everyone, it's been uniquely happy. I am in a right old state of gratitude. Now cooking Lindsay's last meal in the UK and drinking beer.

Danced all night, despite back. Hugh Laurie's band played. Laurie Borg cried again. Stayed till the end. Home four-ish.

APPENDICES

THE PRIZE-WINNING LETTER WRITTEN BY IMOGEN STUBBS
(*See Diaries, 7th April*)

Dear Elinor,

Robert and I have been enjoying a splendid weekend with the Prince Regent, with whom, I declare, I feel quite at home, and who is a veritable gentleman towards we ladies. He has called me 'sumptuous' and 'frivolous' by turns all weekend, and even remarked on my famous curls – enquiring whether 'God did all' or did they require 'feminine assistance'? How we laughed!

My dear Elinor – I feel the time has come to have a little discussion about the past, but before I begin, do tell – how are your precious family? Is poor, pale Marianne happy now with the marvellously competent, mature husband? I shall never forget the pathetic lachrymosity (my! the vocabulary one acquires in 'society') of her warbling, when that wretched scoundrel left her innocent, trusting self for material advantage. Well – he must live with his shame. We can be grateful for that at least. Is darling Margaret behaving herself? I do so miss her mischievous ways, and have quite forgiven her the time when she placed a beetle in my soup, and then laughed fit to burst as I was carried upstairs in a faint. How could she know how close I was to choking to death? How could she know how deeply affected I was by the experience? How could she know at that tender age that one day I might be in a position to offer her assistance financially, or an entry into polite society, and might not care to forget such behaviour? I jest – and for proof, enclose a bonnet-ribbon to prettify that sweet, homely face.

Has Mrs Jennings managed to lose weight, and has your mother gained any? If only a doctor could cut pieces off one person and transfer them to another, how content we should be! For my own part, I should like to have my face pinned into my hair to remove the creases, and restore even more girlish grace than thankfully is still in residence. Robert says I am like a pretty

---

cottage door, with roses growing about it (my curls, you see). He is quite the poet – and outshines that melancholic drear man Cowper any day, don't you think? Enough of *moi*.

Edward looked rather forlorn when we met you in the arcade, I felt. And I see the grey hair is galloping apace. But he is a good soul, and very kind, and I am sure the life of a Rector is nourishing his spirit, if not his body. Our little Alphonse said she thought Uncle Edward 'thutch a thweetheart' (she has an adorable lisp), 'because he hath a thmile like Thuki'. Thuki (Suki) is her pet spaniel (thpaniel) and does indeed resemble Edward – including the hair on his ears, and that silly wart under his chin. Is she not clever to notice the comparison?

Dearest Elinor – I gather you pine for children, and in this area there may be problems. Fear not – you can share my five (especially little Alphonse) and, I do sincerely believe, one can glean as much joy from a pet dog or a garden. Have you tried fennel? I gather this can help fertility, although, perhaps, you are too old to reap the benefits of this particular remedy. Perhaps God will intervene – especially since Edward is in such frequent contact with him!

Oh, I must tell you – the Prince has just popped his head round the corner and invited me for a midnight drive. Should I go? If only you were here to advise me . . . I am in quite a fluster. Do I wear my fur or my velvet? I shall picture your dear self and I am sure the right choice will float across my eyes. I do feel that I have come home here. It is quite odd. Perhaps I was a royal personage in a former life. Whatever – it fits me like a glove.

Now to our discussion. I feel rather frightened – as if I were opening my heart to a governess or to an irritable seagull intent on pecking out my eyes. Not that I intend any comparison – the fault is in my imagination, which Robert says is too fanciful for my own good. No, no – if you were a bird, Elinor, you would be a lovely wise owl a-brooding on your branch – whereas I see myself as more of a Jenny Wren. As for Edward, he is a duck-billed platypus with those absurd flat feet and his honking great nose. How is his sinusitis, by the way? It seemed to preoccupy him a great deal too much for his own good; but it must be awful if one lives in damp conditions, as I fear you do.

When we first met, Elinor, I confided in you (who became like a sister to me) of my engagement to Edward, and the impossible circumstances which surrounded the liaison. Had I known your feelings for him at the time I should never have embarked on such a tactless communication. Indeed, I know you will believe me when I say that such is my nature, I should have renounced him at once had I known this would have given you the happiness you sought. I must therefore chastise you for never conveying your true emotions to me, and choosing to lie to me rather than treat me as your confidante. But I forgive you – and enclose the rather soiled handkerchief which I believe was a great source of concern when, in my innocence, I chanced to have necessity of it. It was given to me by Edward in the foolish passion of his youth which has now waned with age, along with the kerchief.

For my part, I found his brother the man I sought – and will never regret my decision to give my Edward the fate he deserved. Money has never been my concern – how can one miss what one has never known? Although I believe we are not poor, I seek simple pleasures, and look for heaven for my rewards. As for Edward's mother – I need not have feared. She loves me as the daughter she never knew, and has a great weakness for my pastries. She has a great love of wrapping presents, which I share, and many is the happy hour we spend together, wrapping and chatting like schoolgirls.

So I wish you every happiness, Elinor. And never, never feel distressed about your dishonesty towards me, nor your deception of Edward. All is forgiven and forgotten – and love repairs all damage. The worst thing that could befall either yourself or Edward would be to let an oppressed conscience dull your natural charm. Enjoy what life remains to you both, unencumbered by the patter of tiny feet.

Yours lovingly,
　Lucy

PS. Robert sends warm regards to what he humorously calls 'The Wrecktory' (referring, of course, to the tragedy of your poor orchard after the gale).

PPS. Purple is a dainty colour for a skin like yours.

———

Cast
(In order of appearance)

John Dashwood	James Fleet
Mr. Dashwood	Tom Wilkinson
Fanny Dashwood	Harriet Walter
Marianne Dashwood	Kate Winslet
Elinor Dashwood	Emma Thompson
Mrs. Dashwood	Gemma Jones
Edward Ferrars	Hugh Grant
Margaret Dashwood	Emilie François
Mrs. Jennings	Elizabeth Spriggs
Sir John Middleton	Robert Hardy
Thomas	Ian Brimble
Betsy	Isabelle Amyes
Colonel Brandon	Alan Rickman
John Willoughby	Greg Wise
Curate	Alexander John
Charlotte Palmer	Imelda Staunton
Lucy Steele	Imogen Stubbs
Mr. Palmer	Hugh Laurie
Pigeon	Allan Mitchell
Maid to Mrs. Jennings	Josephine Gradwell
Robert Ferrars	Richard Lumsden
Miss Grey	Lone Vidahl
Doctor Harris	Oliver Ford Davies
Mrs. Bunting	Eleanor McCready

THE LOCATIONS

SALTRAM HOUSE. Standing in for the Dashwood family home Norland Park, Saltram House is located at Plympton, not far from Plymouth Hoe where memorials stand to the Pilgrim Fathers and Francis Drake. The house is filled with artwork, including portraits by Sir Joshua Reynolds. Ten of his original paintings, along with priceless works by Italian, Dutch and Flemish masters, cover the walls. Saltram House is owned by the National Trust and is open to the public.

TRAFALGAR HOUSE, near Salisbury, stood in for Sir John Middleton's home, Barton Park. The festive grounds provided the location for the game of lawn bowling played by the Dashwood sisters, and the music room's spectacular murals served as the background for Colonel Brandon's first meeting with Marianne. Presently unoccupied, Trafalgar House was originally given by the government to the family of Lord Nelson.

FLETE ESTATE. Barton Cottage is located on the vast Flete Estate at Holbeton, south Devon. The cottage, which appears modest from the front, is actually a magnificent Edwardian residence when viewed from the side, a fact the filmmakers took pains to conceal. The area is renowned for its wild life, particularly rare birds, a fact of life appreciated more by naturalists than sound recordists.

MONTACUTE HOUSE doubled for the Palmers' estate at Cleveland. Near Yeovil in Somerset, Montacute was built in the late sixteenth century by Sir Edward Phelips, Speaker in the House of Commons and Master of the Rolls. Now a property of the National Trust, Montacute offers a fantastic profusion of gables, obelisks, turrets and secret pavilions.

One of the most striking features of the Montacute grounds is a strange, twisted hedge which the filmmakers nicknamed the 'Brain Hedge'. Deformed long ago by a freeze, and deliberately maintained in this shape ever since, this tall, misshapen hedge offered the filmmakers the perfect background for Marianne's physical and emotional deterioration.

WILTON HOUSE. The Ball visited by the Dashwood sisters was staged at Wilton House, near Salisbury, Wiltshire, a sixteenth-century mansion largely designed by Inigo Jones. Jones's love of theatre is shown in a set of state rooms unparalleled in any other English house. A series of ante-rooms leads to the Cube room (so named for its $40' \times 40' \times 40'$ proportions), followed by the even more spectacular Double Cube ($40' \times 40' \times 80'$), a huge room blazing with gilded swags, garlands, cornices and pediments.

The room is filled with paintings, dominated by a massive portrait by Van Dyck of the Herbert family, who still owns the property. The furniture and mirrors are by Chippendale and William Kent.

Many sovereigns, including the present Queen, have been entertained in this magnificent room, and in wartime, the Normandy invasion was planned in the Double Cube.

MOMPESSON HOUSE. Eighteenth-century Mompesson House, which dominates Choristers' Green in the close of Salisbury Cathedral, doubled for Mrs Jennings's sumptuous London town house. Built in 1701, Mompesson is generally regarded as a perfect complement to the gothic mastery of the cathedral, but the architect and craftsmen who created the house have never been identified. Mompesson House is now owned by the National Trust.

MOTHECOMBE HOUSE, the magnificent Queen Anne manor house owned by farmer, forester and amateur national hunt jockey Anthony Mildmsy White, provided the setting for the drawing room of Mrs Jennings's London house. The stately room provided the backdrop for many important scenes in the film, including Edward's horrified confrontation with Lucy and Elinor.

EMMA THOMPSON won an Academy Award for Best Actress in 1992 for her portrayal of Margaret Schlegel in *Howards End* and was nominated twice in 1993 for her leading role in *The Remains of the Day* and her supporting role in *In the Name of the Father.*

Sense and Sensibility is her first screenplay.

Before graduating from Cambridge University in 1982 with a degree in English Literature, Thompson acted for three years with the Footlights at the Edinburgh Fringe; with Cambridge's first all-female revue *Woman's Hour,* which she co-wrote, co-produced and co-directed; and in her first solo show, *Short Vehicle.*

In London, Thompson starred opposite Robert Lindsay in the hit revival of *Me and My Girl*, and opposite Kenneth Branagh in John Osborne's *Look Back in Anger*, directed by Dame Judi Dench. For the Renaissance Theatre Company World Tour, she was directed by Branagh as the Fool in *King Lear,* and as Helena in *A Midsummer Night's Dream.* A BBC broadcast of the early Cambridge Footlights led to many other comedy appearances for Thompson, which culminated in *The Emma Thompson Special.* More dramatic work began with roles in the BBC six-hour mini-series *Tutti Frutti* and the seven-hour BBC series *Fortunes of War,* for which she won the BAFTA Best Actress award.

Thompson's additional film credits include *Junior, Much Ado About Nothing, Henry V, Dead Again, Peter's Friends,* and *Impromptu.* Most recently, she played the title role in Christopher Hampton's *Carrington,* which won a Special Jury Prize at the 1995 Cannes Festival.

LINDSAY DORAN was born in Los Angeles and worked as a studio executive with Embassy Pictures and Paramount Pictures for ten years before becoming president of Sydney Pollack's Mirage Productions.

After producing Kenneth Branagh's *Dead Again* and Edward Zwick's *Leaving Normal*, she served as executive producer on Pollack's *The Firm* and his most recent film, *Sabrina*. She was executive in charge of production on Rob Reiner's *This is Spinal Tap*, and executive producer on Mirage's critically acclaimed anthology series, *Fallen Angels*, for Showtime Television.